Praise for Twenty for Break

"Ready for a vocational change in your life? Is corporate drudgery eroding your energy? Always toyed with owning your own business?

Pat Materka, innkeeper of the #1 TripAdvisor rated Bed & Breakfast in Ann Arbor, Michigan takes you down the discovery path of this rewarding lifestyle, including:

- Inspiring confidence that "I can do this!"
- Leading you through the essentials of hospitality
- Entertaining with personal anecdotes…each with a "moral to the story"

Straight talk about enjoying the life-long dream many Americans covet… and what it takes to make the dream a reality."

> —Scott Bushnell, co-owner with his wife Marilyn, of
> Bushnell & Bushnell Services, a real estate and
> consulting company serving the Innkeeping industry

"…An accurate and honest must-read for anyone interested in the profession of innkeeping. This is not another how-to book. It goes beyond that with an inside look at the unexpected in the day-to-day personal realities of being an innkeeper and provides insights on how to manage those challenges successfully."

> —Mary White, President of BnBFinder.com and
> author of *Running a Bed and Breakfast For Dummies*

"If you have you ever wondered what goes on behind the scenes of a bed and breakfast, this is the book for you. Pat Materka has written in frank detail, but with a great sense of humor, the ups and downs of this interesting endeavor. Practitioners will appreciate the hints, but the merely curious will also enjoy living vicariously in a bed and breakfast."

> —Grace Shackman, historian, journalist,
> and author of *Ann Arbor Observed*

"Not only a practical guide to the nuts and bolts of running an inn—from figuring out whether it really might suit you, to details that save energy, time, and money while maximizing guests' experiences and gaining glowing reviews and repeat visits.

…The anecdotes lit by Pat's sunny disposition make this a great read even if you haven't the slightest interest in running, or even visiting, a bed and breakfast. Heart-warming and hilarious.

—Joan Reisman-Brill, columnist, "The Humanist Dilemma"

"Every aspect of running a successful B&B is laid out honestly. Pat has housed, fed, entertained, and cleaned up after hundreds of happy house guests at her cozy bed and breakfast in Ann Arbor, Michigan. Now she's sharing her tips, lessons and insights in this entertaining, informative look behind the scenes. Readers will fall in love with Pat's warmth and sense of humor, as she dispenses wisdom on marriage and marmalade, etiquette and egg dishes,… all of the best ways to make fortunate travelers feel at home and part of her extended family and fascinating life.

—Priscilla Warner, New York Times best-selling author of *Learning to Breathe* and co-author of *The Faith Club*

"Whether an aspiring innkeeper, bed-and-breakfast aficionado, or someone who appreciates a heartwarming tale, you'll love this book with practical tips, recipes, and stories including how Pat and Bob met insurmountable challenges with the support of their family, friends, and community."

—Anita LeBlanc, journalist and President, The Write Word

"Pat Materka's delightful guide to inn-keeping is part memoir, part cautionary tale, and wholly inspiring. Her ever positive outlook is evidenced throughout, making this a fun read for everyone - not just those interested in running a B&B."

—Inger Schultz

"… A must read for those who love staying in B&Bs or have ever thought about owning one. Pat shares lessons learned during more than fourteen years as an innkeeper, along with humorous accounts of the joys and challenges of caring for and feeding thousands of guests each year."

—Mary Jo Frank

"Part instruction manual, part memoir, *Twenty for Breakfast* is for aspiring innkeepers and travelers who embrace the serendipity of life. The book is filled with helpful tips for starting an inn including location selection, managing the daily housekeeping, and handling mishaps. More importantly it lays bare the essence of what the best bed and breakfasts and innkeepers are made of. By intertwining personal stories with an intimate look at innkeeping, Pat shows us that a generous heart, resiliency, and a love for human connection are what makes an inn a home and what makes a heart a soul."

—Hilary MacPhail

"Peek behind the curtains of this five-star rated boutique bed & breakfast, steps from the central campus of the University of Michigan. Follow the owners as they research, purchase and manage this delightful B&B. Meet the parade of guests, and navigate the highs and lows of this unique enterprise"

—Bill Bradley, Author of the regional best-selling
Pirate's Guide to Lake St. Clair & Surrounding Waters

"Twenty for Breakfast combines a witty and sometimes poignant memoir with a solid, practical guide to running a B&B that will appeal to new and veteran innkeepers as well as anyone who thinks "maybe someday."

An experienced business owner and public relations professional who offered sound time management advice in her first book, *Time In, Time Out, Time Enough,* Pat now chronicles her and husband Bob's transition from happy semi-retirees in the warm environs of Laguna Beach, California, to owners of a not-exactly-flourishing B&B in decidedly-less-balmy Ann Arbor, Michigan. In fact, Pat and Bob had raised their family in Ann Arbor, where Pat worked for the University of Michigan for many years. Their new adventure was also a homecoming.

Pat's organizational skills, attention to detail, creativity, warmth, and sense of humor, combined with Bob's experience as an early technology entrepreneur, were invaluable assets in their new career. Still, the transition was not always easy, and along the way they encountered business setbacks and personal tragedy. But they persevered, and the inn is often full to capacity. As Pat's long-time friend and colleague, I am not surprised to see her look forward, not back, plunging into new territory with her indomitable blend of optimism and just plain grit. Her story is an inspiration and a "how-to" manual for moving on to that next career or life passage."

—Judy Phair, President of PhairAdvantage Communications LLC
and National President (2005) Public Relations Society of America.

Twenty for Breakfast

by

Pat Roessle Materka

ISBN: 978-0-9986711-1-6

Pat Materka
Ann Arbor Bed and Breakfast
921 E. Huron
Ann Arbor, MI 48104
www.20forBreakfast.com

Dedicated to Marc, who always said,
"Someday I'm going to run a B&B when I'm,
you know, a lot older."

CONTENTS

Contents

Channeling Bob Newhart

It was a balmy spring day in southern California. My husband Bob and I, on vacation, were wheeling a cart through the produce aisles of Trader Joe's outside Laguna Beach. Bob, wearing his iconic navy blue University of Michigan sweatshirt, drew the attention of another pair of shoppers. The friendly couple who looked to be about our age in their mid-sixties, struck up a conversation, telling us that they too are U-M alumni. They began reminiscing about their fond memories of going to school in Ann Arbor. When we mentioned that we still lived there, they raised the inevitable question: "What do you do?"

"We own the Ann Arbor Bed and Breakfast."

The woman's eyes widened, and she broke into a huge smile. "Running a bed and breakfast?" she began. "Omigosh, that is my..."

And, I waited for her to say "lifelong dream."

Instead, she declared "... worst nightmare!"

"Having people in your house all the time," she shuddered. "Total strangers. Catering to their every need. And then you have to get up in the morning and *fix them breakfast!*"

Wow, I remember thinking, she did have a point. Stated like that, innkeeping does sound like a peculiar choice of occupation.

More often, we innkeepers encounter the opposite impression. People tend to romanticize running a bed and breakfast, conjuring up a lofty image of working from home in luxuriant surroundings. We get to meet fascinating people and engage them in riveting conversations, as our bank balance grows with each swipe of the credit card at check-in.

Think of the classic TV sitcom *Newhart,* set in a Vermont Inn. Did you ever see the lead characters making a bed?

Of course, neither extreme is the true picture. Let's call it "the snapshot versus the movie."

The *snapshot* version of what we do tells one tiny piece of the story. Like any photo, it's static. Whether idyllic or horrifying, the snapshot captures a single facet of running a B&B. It's as if you are watching an epic film on DVD and press the pause button, freezing the action to a single frame. It leaves a single image but it doesn't divulge the plot or all of the characters. It's far from the full story.

Now press play. The *movie* unfolds a more nuanced and balanced picture of innkeeping: the great fun of outfitting the guestrooms; the drudgery of keeping them dusted. Guests who enrich your life with their warmth and appreciation; guests who cancel at the last minute, or never show up at all. It's the six-room-wedding booking during off-season that covers the mortgage payment; it's the furnace that fails on that same weekend. And you can be sure that if your furnace, plumbing, or any appliance chooses to fail, it will always, *always,* happen on the weekend.

The reality of running a B&B is excitement and exhaustion and everything in between. It's like no other occupation. It isn't a job; it's a lifestyle.

Twenty for Breakfast is about that lifestyle. It celebrates the pleasure of creating a welcoming environment, making a difference to someone, and being of service. Am I sounding too rapturous? It is also about the mistakes and catastrophes. Of course, we never refer to anything that goes wrong as a "mistake" in this business. It is merely a "valuable learning experience."

While other trade books focus on the economic aspects of running a B&B, such as writing a business plan, optimizing search engines, and designing a website, *Twenty for Breakfast* focuses on the social aspects. Innkeeping is ultimately about people: greeting, feeding, accommodating, appeasing, and appreciating them—and that includes your partner, staff, and innkeeper colleagues as well as your guests. Synthesizing fourteen years of anecdotes and "aha" moments, *Twenty for Breakfast* is an inside view of the bed and breakfast life.

ONE

Inn-The Beginning

Astrology, fortune telling, clairvoyance—many people scoff at such things, but I like to keep an open mind. Years ago, a self-professed psychic insisted she saw a "fluffy white animal" romping around the yard with Jasmine, our black lab. "You're mistaken," I assured her. "We have only one pet." Two weeks later we were in New Orleans to visit my brother Rex whose Old English sheepdog had just delivered ten puppies. "And you've found homes for all of them?" I asked when he met us at the airport. "Nope, we have one little female left." You can already guess who came home with us.

So when I left my job at the University of Michigan in 2000 and the same person predicted that I would return to an earlier profession, I figured she meant that I'd take up freelance writing, which I'd pursued in my twenties. I'd sold articles to some national magazines when my kids were in preschool. Or, maybe she meant I'd publish another book. That sounded even better.

It turned out she was referring to how I spent the summer of 1964, following my sophomore year of college. I was a cabin maid at Old Faithful Lodge in Yellowstone Park. Apparently I was about to go back to making beds for a living—as an innkeeper at a bed and breakfast.

What brought us to this strange juncture? My husband Bob and I met on April Fools' Day, 1967 when we were both twenty-three. He was a software guru in those days when computers—he worked on one called a PDP5—filled an entire room. I was an *Ann Arbor News* reporter assigned to the police beat and the garden page. After our children, Shannon and Marc, were born, I chose the slower-paced realm of public relations and fundraising at the University of Michigan, which allowed time for freelance writing and running a weekend antique business. In my 30s, I published a book called *Time In, Time Out, Time Enough: A Time Management Guide for Women,* leading to a third part-time career teaching time management workshops. All of these activities continued after our kids went off to college and began lives of their own.

The idea of opening a bed and breakfast had come up in conversation now and then, but always in the context of "one-of-these-days, maybe…" It was a remote fantasy, like snorkeling with giant turtles in the Galapagos. Both thoughts sat squarely on the back burner.

The truth is we had rarely stayed at B&Bs, since most of our travels took us to the homes of family and friends. We loved having houseguests in return, even though our 1842 farmhouse had just one bathroom and three tiny bedrooms. No matter, our oversized red corduroy couch was as deep as a rollaway and twice as comfortable.

And we were the ones among our circle of friends who most often hosted the dinner parties, the baby showers, the annual office picnic. For ten years, we invited everyone we knew to our annual June strawberry festival and badminton tournament, which grew so popular that some people told us that they scheduled their summer vacations so as not to miss the event. Our friends became friends with one another, and the circles grew. We sought any excuse for bringing people together.

Then on February 29, 2000 (Leap Day, appropriately), I retired from my position as director of development and alumni relations for the U-M School of Kinesiology at the same time Bob finished up his last consulting gig. The stars aligned. Our children were grown. The stock market was (at that brief moment) soaring, making us feel dizzily rich. We bought a condo in southern California and tried living bicoastal between Laguna Beach and our hometown of Ann Arbor.

But retirement made us restless. We didn't own a sailboat and we don't play golf. We needed a project.

As if it had been patiently waiting its turn to get our attention, the B&B notion rose to the fore. In 2002, while visiting relatives in Florida over Thanksgiving, we made a short getaway to Key West. Along with sparkling white sand and an azure ocean, this southern-most island had close to fifty B&Bs, each one as charming as the next. We stayed at the historic whitewashed and gabled Conch House off downtown's Duval Street. Relaxing on the breezy veranda with a good book and a glass of wine, I thought, *I could live like this.*

I could welcome friendly guests, set out a fresh healthy breakfast, and collect seashells while strolling the beach in my abundant spare time. I could trade snow boots for sandals, and glow with a golden suntan all year long.

Bob too saw the possibilities. A bed and breakfast seemed like an inventive way to merge his computer skills (we'd be first on the block to offer on-line reservations and free wireless internet) and my interest in cooking. He tossed out marketing ideas. I conjured up recipes involving eggs and cheese.

It's a long winding drive from Key West to Miami, and by the end of three hours' non-stop discussion, we were convinced that owning a B&B was our destiny. It would be more than a project. It would be an adventure.

Are you nuts? Are you crazy?

Soon after, we had dinner with our Chicago friends Bonnie and Jerry Spinazzi, who deflated our enthusiasm like a hatpin puncturing a balloon.

"Bad idea," they said, shaking their heads. "Running a B&B is incredibly confining. Two of our best friends started a B&B eighteen months ago and they have never been able to take a vacation," Bonnie told us. "They can't even get away for our daughter's wedding—and they are her godparents!"

On we talked. But instead of getting discouraged, we grew more excited. A brazen plan developed. What if their friends took the opportunity to go to the wedding and let us run the inn their absence? We could find out what it's really like before making a life-long commitment. Screwing up courage, I cold called Marge and Dom Trumfio, the owners of the Water's Edge Bed and Breakfast in Lake Geneva, Wisconsin. Referencing our mutual friends, the Spinazzis, I proposed that we would take care of their inn so that they could attend the wedding. "We're happy to work for free," I emphasized, "in exchange for the learning experience." They listened with interest. By the end of an hour's phone conversation, they agreed to the plan. "I think your call is a gift," Marge told me. Clearly this exchange could be win-win for all of us.

TWO

Try It Before You Buy It

Every parent recalls the anxiety of turning over the watch of his or her firstborn to a neophyte babysitter; especially the slightly spacey fourteen-year-old neighbor who admits this is a first-time experience. Marge and Dom Trumfio must surely have felt the same about leaving their "baby" with Bob and me for nine days that included the 2003 season grand-opener, Memorial Day weekend.

They understood that we had neither courses nor credentials in the hospitality industry. Yet our phone conversations had created a strong sense of rapport. Besides, we were the ticket to their long overdue vacation. By the time May rolled around, they were not only set for the wedding, but had extended their itinerary to include visits with friends up and down California's west coast.

Bob and I drove to Lake Geneva from Ann Arbor for hands-on training two days before their departure. The four of us hit it off instantly, which is no surprise given our common interest in innkeeping. Whatever reservations or concerns any of us may have had about this trade-off, we masked them with enthusiasm and confidence.

Dom was a practicing dentist who loves to cook. Marge was an interior designer whose verve and style were reflected in each of their seven colorful rooms and suites. The house was spacious and gracious, with an intriguing past. Built in the late 1800s, the Water's Edge became the getaway place of Chicago gangster Bugs Moran during the 1930s. "Guests love to hear about the history of the place where they are staying," Marge informed us, as she led us down to the Inn's lower level. Here you could almost envision the smoke-filled room, the poker tables where the mobsters gambled and counted their bootleg money. She showed us the drive-through vault where cash had been unloaded from vehicles. This was so cool! We would get to practice being tour guides as well as innkeepers. Gangland Chicago lives on at the Water's Edge Bed & Breakfast, especially—with its barred windows and corner slot machine—in the Bugs Moran suite.

Our orientation continued as we toured the remaining six guestrooms, one of which was reserved for us. Like most innkeepers, the Trumfios have their own private suite within the B&B where they can escape as needed. We checked out the linen closet and the laundry room and the cabinet drawers filled with paisley place mats and matching napkins, all neatly pressed and folded into squares and triangles. The table was already set for the next day's breakfast.

The Trumfios had supplied us with a well-stocked fridge, freezer, and pantry, but in this business, you're sure to run short of bananas and bread. So once they'd showed us the lay of the inn, we set off to learn the lay of the land. Driving around Lake Geneva, Marge and Dom took us on the route to the nearest supermarket, pointed out their favorite restaurants, and made sure we could find the local emergency health clinic. By late afternoon, it was back to the inn to greet incoming guests and begin prepping a spinach-and-egg casserole for the next morning's breakfast. It was past noon when Bob suddenly turned to me and said, "What day is this?" We were so absorbed in the learning process that I had forgotten his May 17th birthday, for the first time in thirty-five years of marriage.

By six o'clock the next morning, we were at work alongside Dom in the kitchen. The pace was busy but not frantic. The aroma of sizzling bacon was intoxicating. From the dining room came the pleasant banter of gathering guests as I set about my assigned task, slicing a chilled stick of butter into perfectly even quarter-inch thick squares. *So this is all it takes to run a B&B,* I thought to myself as I lined up the row of butter pats like soldiers on the ceramic tray. We were ready to fly solo.

The following day our hosts were off to the airport, arming us with phone numbers, detailed instruction sheets, and votes of confidence. "This'll cure you," Dom cheerfully assured us, "of wanting to run a B&B on a full-time basis."

But it didn't. We loved every minute of the experience.

We loved taking charge of this local landmark and sharing its colorful history. We enjoyed greeting total strangers, learning about their interests, making them feel welcome. Even the most mundane tasks, like stripping and re-making beds and setting the table, were fun and engaging because I got to use someone else's beautiful belongings. It was like a grown-up version of playing house.

And we had plenty of support. Diane, their reliable housekeeper, arrived daily to handle the heavy cleaning and laundry. Diane was also a gifted photographer who had created note cards from the photos she'd taken of sunsets over the lake. There is something about a B&B environment that inspires creativity in everyone associated with it.

Every incoming phone call related to a potential room reservation carried an element of suspense and posed a challenge. Did we have the accommodations they were seeking? Would the caller book the room? Would we close the sale?

We tracked the reservations in a thick yellow three-ring binder notebook. (In 2003 many inns had not yet converted to computer-based reservation systems.) When we left during the day to buy groceries or run other errands, we forwarded the Water's Edge phone to Bob's cell phone so we would not miss any calls. The reservation notebook always came with us, like a trusty sidekick.

At Lake Geneva, we learned an important aspect of running a B&B on a waterfront (and this holds true for anyone running an inn near a national park, or next to a ski lift): weather matters. Like merchants waiting impatiently for a revenue boost on Black Friday, innkeepers count on filling their rooms on holiday weekends. But as Memorial Day drew closer, we noticed half of our rooms remained empty. We realized that was directly correlated to the chilly weekend temperature forecast.

Running a B&B does not ensure a reliable income stream. People will make reservations weeks in advance if they're coming for a concert or a conference. But if they're just looking to relax and enjoy the outdoors, they'll wait to book at the last minute, making sure the forecast calls for sunshine.

This story, and thus this chapter, has a happy ending. The weather warmed up, the rooms filled to capacity, Marge and Dom came back refreshed, and we returned to Ann Arbor more motivated than ever to launch our own hospitality venue.

Here are a few more ideas and insights we gained from our inn-sitting experience at the Water's Edge. While neither surprising nor profound, these first impressions cemented the notion that running our own B&B would be realistic and rewarding. We had lots to learn, but here were some benchmarks on where to begin:

- Innkeeping is not about you; it's about the guests. And the good news is, people who choose a B&B are almost universally gregarious, adventurous, and agreeable. I sense they come with more modest expectations than folks who seek out an elite resort. (And we innkeepers do relish exceeding those expectations!)

- Think big. Large bottles of herbal shampoo and bath gel on a shower rack are a viable alternative to those ubiquitous little bottles we associate with hotels. They are much less costly and look generous and luxuriant.

- Anticipate every guest need. In addition to the expected soap, lotion, shampoo and conditioner, stock every kind of amenity your guest might need, including toothbrush and toothpaste; sewing notions; band-aids and first aid supplies; razors and shaving cream, shower caps, pens and paper, and so on. We ultimately designated a help-yourself place for these items in the B&B's common area. We call it "the table of anything you may have left behind, or may have been confiscated by airport security."

- On the same note, offer a selection of fresh fruit, home-baked cookies, packaged snacks, hot and cold beverages, and water. Never charge for any of these extras. The cost of providing complementary amenities is exceeded by the good will they generate.

- Plan ahead. The more you prepare the night before, the easier goes your morning. (You'll read more on the theme of prepping ahead in the chapters to come.)

- In addition to the entrée you serve, always offer a selection of granola and cereals on a sideboard. Many people prefer a cold breakfast, and…

- Practically everyone likes Cheerios.

THREE

Location, Location, Location

Our stint at the Water's Edge clarified what kind of inn we were seeking: it had to have at least five or more bedrooms, with an existing clientele and track record. We were nearing sixty and did not want lose valuable years of the B&B experience by starting an inn from scratch. We figured it might take up to a year to check out inns for sale from the Carolinas to (why not dream big?) coastal California. After thirty-seven Michigan winters I was ready for any place south. Tropical might just be the ticket.

Three days into our one-year plan, our Realtor friend Ann Marie Kotre mentioned that a B&B was for sale right in our hometown of Ann Arbor. This did not fit my plan for a warmer climate. But the search had to begin somewhere. What could it hurt to see it?

Two hours later, we were signing a sales offer.

During all of the years we'd lived in the city, I'd never paid much notice to the building marked "Bed and Breakfast on Campus." It sat on Huron street, one of the city's busiest arteries. Driving along Huron, you are watching the oncoming traffic, not gazing at architecture. Now we surveyed this odd structure that resembled a Swiss chalet, its dramatic A-frame roof overhanging tall

One of the first things Marge Trumflo taught me is one I've never forgotten. When guests arrive, greet them by saying "Welcome to our home." the word "home" underscores the difference between a B&B and an impersonal hotel.

windows and a wrap-around balcony. Built in 1962, it looked like an out-of-place ski lodge on the block of 1920s Dutch colonials converted to chicken coops of student housing. It certainly didn't fit most people's image of a B&B, which is a gabled and gothic Victorian.

The building was originally designed as four apartments—one large and three small. Entering from the covered parking lot, two flights of stairs led to the spacious sunlit main floor residence, that featured a brick-walled fireplace, a spiral staircase to the third level, and a sunken living room. A campus bookstore owner, Fred Ulrich, had designed his dream house as one large living space for himself and his wife and daughter, with three small add-on apartments that he could rent to friends and employees. "Daddy grew up during the Depression," his daughter Sandra explained to us when we met her years later. "Even though his business was prosperous, he liked the security of an added income."

Speaking of security, there was even a fallout shelter in the basement. The house had been designed during the Cold War era, when Americans were obsessed over the threat of a Russian nuclear attack. (It's hard to imagine which would be worse—radiation, or waiting days or weeks for the air to clear in a 10×10 foot windowless concrete room.) The fallout shelter has since been cheerfully repurposed for storage.

In 1962, the property was truly avant-garde. In 2003, with its colorless walls and faded grey carpeting, it looked tired and dated. The B&B was being sold "turnkey," which means fully furnished. I calculated how quickly I would turn the furniture over to charity.

But, oh, the potential! The three small apartments could be configured as six separate guestrooms, giving us nine in total, each with its own private en suite bathroom. Up the spiral staircase was a solarium with skylights where we could create our own living space. Our friend Gary Elling, a civil engineer, extolled the concrete and steel construction. And the place came with nine slots of adjacent covered parking—an unheard-of asset next to a university campus.

We walked from room to room, mesmerized by the possibilities. Location, location, location, the three points that drive any real estate decision, are even more critical when you're buying property as a source of income. The University of Michigan draws tens of thousands of visitors, from researchers and recruiters to parents and prospective students. The campus was literally across the street. Who *wouldn't* want to stay here?

My vision of a B&B flanked by billowing palm trees was fading like a mirage. Instead, I was adding up all of the good reasons to stay in Ann Arbor. We had a history here and a broad support network. One of the most essential would prove to be our son Marc, then thirty, who ran his own painting/ remodeling business. Rather than strike out for exotic new locales, maybe it was better to embrace the old adage: bloom where you are planted.

A year later, flipping through an architectural magazine, I ran across the term *Mid-Century Modern.* In the illustrations, I recognized our pitched ceilings, interior brick walls, spiral staircase, and sunken living room. With raised awareness and renewed appreciation, I realized I had been wrong in my first impression. Our 1962 home was not "dated"—it was *vintage.*

Given that Bob and I became innkeepers based more on a hunch than homework, one might say we were lucky to find such a good fit. Lucky because once you've begun taking dozens of reservations six months into the future, innkeeping is not a simple job to quit! It's not a matter of calling the boss and giving two weeks' notice.

Ultimately, I am not sure luck is a factor. It's a little like parenthood. Once you make the commitment, you just throw aside expectations and focus on doing your best at whatever it takes to make it a success.

Don't Do As I Did; Do As I Say

We have never regretted our impulsiveness. But would I recommend it? Would I urge you to go on a blind date and then wrap up the evening by getting married?

Buying an inn is a gigantic commitment, not just to a place but to a lifestyle. Move cautiously, do plenty of research, and enjoy the learning process.

If you want to become an innkeeper:

- Stay in as many B&Bs as possible and study the surroundings. Think about what you might do differently, and what you'd do the same.

- Talk to the owners about what they like and dislike about their chosen occupation.

- Volunteer to pitch in at a local B&B to get a sense of the daily routine.

- Join the Professional Association of Innkeepers International (PAII), and the recently formed Association of Independent Hospitality Professionals (AIHP). Check out their websites and consider attending their national conferences. These organizations also offer informative newsletters, webinars, and member forums.

- Enroll in one of the many regional workshops for aspiring innkeepers. You'll find them advertised on the AIHP or PAII websites. Prospective innkeeper courses are also offered by the B&B Team (bbteam.com) and some state B&B organizations. These courses are a reality check, not a sales pitch. Instructors report that more than half of the participants in these courses decide *not* to pursue this goal.

- Read how-to books on the topic. You'll find a list of Recommended Reading in the Appendix.

FOUR

Hitting the Ground Running, Without a Map

With our offer accepted, we spent the summer of 2003 negotiating with banks on mortgage rates and exploring Small Business Administration (SBA) loan options, the details of which do not make for a riveting read. Besides, the financial industry and the economy has changed so drastically during the past decade that our experience has little relevance in today's market.

Let's skip to the topic of names instead of numbers. Like expectant parents, we debated over what we should call our new inn. The current name, The Bed and Breakfast on Campus, seemed prosaic. How about the Purple Moon? The Flying Elephant? I am embarrassed to admit it took us three months to come up with the obvious. What were we? Where were we? By simply calling ourselves the Ann Arbor Bed and Breakfast we landed on top of every alphabetical listing and Google internet search.

On Monday September 8, 2003 we signed the papers, moved into one of the empty guestrooms, and tore off to the supermarket. Wheeling two jumbo shopping carts, we each set off in different directions. Bob loaded his cart with brooms, mops, cleaning supplies, squirt soaps, and paper products. I stocked up on food from the bakery aisle, produce section, and dairy case. Little did I know that this marathon shopping expedition was not, as I might have imagined, a one-off event. It would replay again and again, and even to this day, shopping for food and cleaning supplies remains a daily part of the B&B life. When you're feeding and housing an average of ten to twenty

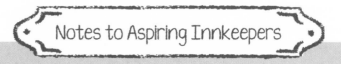

Notes to Aspiring Innkeepers

What's In a Name?

When my friend and fellow innkeeper Sarah Okuyama decided to turn her Ann Arbor home into a B&B, her daughters took it as a joke. "You should call it the Burnt Toast Inn!" they teased.

So Sarah, with easy good humor, did exactly that. It's no surprise that quite a few of her guests say they chose her B&B because they were attracted to the whimsical name and curious about its ambiance. Like a provocative book title or a new product brand, your B&B name is one of your key marketing tools. Choose one that is simple, memorable and evocative. And (no offense to zinnias and zebras), make sure the first letter ranks near the top of the alphabet.

adult lodgers, you'd be surprised how quickly you run out of essentials. We'll explore this theme further in Chapter 8, "Extreme Shopping."

That evening we put away the food and fell asleep early, exhausted but exhilarated. The next morning, we greeted four startled people who had begun their stay at the B&B several days earlier. "Hi," we announced. "We're the new owners." They had no idea of the transition that was taking place, but they seemed genuinely pleased to be a part of it.

Krishna Ghimire was among that first week's guests, visiting the U-M Population Center on behalf of a research project in Nepal, India. Eight years later, we connected on Facebook, where I now see photos and updates on his two children. "Do you remember anything about your stay with us?" I asked him recently, since those early days were a blur to me. "I remember feeling well treated and getting a really good breakfast," he replied. "You were both working very hard moving things around to make them better. I remember you lent me your cell phone for making an international call and insisted on not charging for it. I thought that was awesome."

I easily fell into the routine of setting out an eight o'clock breakfast for Krishna and the other B&B occupants, who were all visiting lecturers or researchers from various university departments.

But how to reach the four Chinese doctors who were here for the U-M's five-day Temporal Bone Course? They bolted off to the classroom at 7:00 a.m. Tuesday without even a backward glance. On Wednesday morning I called after them, waving a banana, but they looked at me in confusion. Clearly they didn't speak English. I concluded they didn't want breakfast.

Thursday morning, I was preparing food for Krishna and four other guests when one of the Chinese otolaryngologists cautiously entered the kitchen. He pointed at the frying pan. "Sausage?" he asked. "Yes," I nodded, gesturing that it was intended for him. Suddenly his three colleagues appeared. "Sausage?" they repeated. I whipped out four plates and piled them with sausage and eggs. Within minutes, all four were seated at the table, eating like locusts. They devoured everything I'd prepared for the rest of the household.

Lesson learned in running a B&B: Expect the unexpected.

Here's what I learned over the course of those frenzied but fun early weeks. If your guests requested breakfast at nine, they'll show up at eight. If you've baked your signature quiche, they'll just be having cereal, thanks. If they forgot to mention they're lactose intolerant, you can bet you'll open the cupboard and find you're out of soymilk.

If you are an aspiring innkeeper who thrives on routine and predictability, look for a different occupation.

On the other hand, maybe you're like Jennifer Hobson, who stayed at our B&B on her wedding night and sent me a thank you note a few days later. "If you ever need help," she wrote, "I live nearby. I would LOVE to be involved in an operation like yours!!"

Did you see those capital letters and exclamation points? There's no quality in a potential employee that impresses me more than enthusiasm. I immediately invited the sparkly-eyed bride back over for further discussion.

"What draws me to the innkeeping business is that I never know what will happen next," she explained to me. "I thrive under pressure and often seek it out because in the end, I learn that I can handle it and make it through any situation just fine."

We hired Jennifer to manage the B&B whenever we needed to take a trip out of town. She became our go-to innsitter, overseeing everything from taking reservations to shopping and cooking, in the same way that we had run the Water's Edge B&B in its owners' absence. Spunky and competent, Jennifer went on to manage an upscale inn in Savannah, GA when her husband Mike began graduate school at the Savannah College of Art and Design. Though she has explored many other career paths, Jennifer still has a special affinity for the B&B business.

"I never know what will be at the bottom of the rabbit hole. And that's the way I like it. Life would be boring without all kinds of things falling apart while still being wonderful. *In Omnia Paratus,"* she concluded. For those of us who didn't take Latin 101, those words are roughly translated as "ready for anything."

Barreling Ahead

Ready for anything does not describe how I felt during our opening weeks. "Do you have any glasses for the orange juice?" a guest would ask hopefully. Even after making a checklist, I could overlook the most obvious elements of the most elementary task I had—setting out breakfast. Fortunately, our B&B seemed to attract undemanding, appreciative folks who cut us quite a bit of slack as we clambered up the steep learning curve.

Never knowing what to expect (except the unexpected), I was caught off guard when a couple checked in early for one of our first football weekends.

We chatted as I led them past an open doorway displaying a king-sized bedroom, leather chairs, and sliding glass doors opening onto a spacious balcony. Then I ushered them into their assigned room, which had a queen bed, no balcony, and an ambiance most charitably described as "cozy."

"Why can't we have that other room we walked past, the larger one?" the wife demanded.

"Well, you see, someone else has booked that room this weekend."

"But we were here first!"

Totally flustered, I managed to explain that the larger room was already reserved. It wasn't a matter of first come, first served. In the end, they understood, and have returned numerous times (to the larger room). Like many recurring guests, they've come to be friends, but I've never forgotten our first encounter.

That first fall, I emailed a couple who were visiting their daughter on campus, asking if they had any special requests for breakfast. "I eat pretty much anything," Glen replied. "But I asked my wife, and she suggested: whole grain organic cereal, nonfat organic yogurt, organic raspberries, black organic decaffeinated tea…" Whoa, what was I getting into? (Can you guess that these two lived in Southern California?)

I braced myself for someone thin, fit, gorgeous, and very very picky. Leonie was all three of the first but not at all the fourth. She was just politely responding to my question. I now know that conversationally asking someone "what would you like to eat?" is to open a Pandora's recipe box. Brace yourself for an order of Belgian waffles or Eggs Benedict.

On the other hand, it's important and practical to ask, "What *can't* you eat?" People are allergic to an astonishing variety of food items, from tree nuts to kiwi (not to mention goose down in our premium duvets and pillows and the chemicals used in certain cleaning products). "Are there any allergies or food preferences we should know about?" became part of our reservation script. A head's up in advance prevents problems later. People always appreciate being asked.

"How's It Going...Really?"

People were finding our website, and every call seemed like a gift, a stamp of approval. We sent an email blast to the administrative assistants of every university dean and department head announcing our existence and inviting them to an open house. Passersby saw our sign, rang the bell, and asked for a tour. Within a week of opening, we booked every room for the following spring's graduation.

Who was not calling, I noticed, were our friends. Effusive in their enthusiasm when we announced we were buying a B&B—"Oh wow! That is so perfect for you!"—they were now conspicuously silent. I knew why. No one wanted to ask, "how's it going?" for fear they would find out it was not going well.

I'll be honest; running a business with my husband (or any husband, or any other fellow human) seemed fraught with risk. Here's a shocking disclosure: we don't agree about everything. We've all heard many stories of partnerships that ended badly (Luci and Desi; Simon and Garfunkel) because familiarity finally bred contempt. Could we handle the stress of extreme togetherness? What if running a B&B together became our undoing?

But we'd recently weathered something more difficult—the void of retirement. If we could handle the challenge of doing *nothing* (or at least not enough) together, surely we could manage the frenzy of staying busy.

The truth was, we were—and still are—having a blast. It certainly gave us plenty to talk about.

> Our friends were supportive of our B&B venture, but certainly not envious. Mary Joscelyn and Pringle Smith, though two of the most friendly and generous women I know, nudged each other and smirked. "If we were running it," they laughed. "we'd call it BYOB–Bring your own breakfast!"

And what's our favorite topic? More often than not it's our guests, who are consistently entertaining. Like nearly every innkeeper on the planet, we genuinely like interacting with people. Which, as you size up the qualities required for being an innkeeper, is the only trait that's non-negotiable.

"I'll bet you're really busy on football weekends" was a comment we heard often, and still do. Wrong. We are busy *all* the time. Many inns are seasonal and tied to tourism, whereas visitors have reasons to come to the university year-round. Our guests include visiting lecturers, research collaborators, conference attendees, faculty recruits, alumni, and parents and grandparents visiting students. The university is not the only draw—so is Ann Arbor, which is frequently cited on various top ten lists for everything ranging from "best cities for singles" to "most affordable retirement." Even during the decade's economic downturn, our weekends were filled with couples from a sixty-mile radius enjoying a getaway to Ann Arbor's lively theaters and restaurants.

Parents bringing their high school-aged kids for a campus tour have become one of my favorite guest categories. The kinds of families who bring students to visit the U-M (and other) campuses are congenial and close-knit. The teenagers are excited and motivated, not sullen. If they apply to Michigan and are accepted, they are invited to the Campus Day recruiting event. If they decide to enroll, we often see them and their parents for orientation, move-in, parents weekend, birthdays, recitals, and other events over the four years of their college life. By graduation, I feel like a doting aunt, highly invested in their career paths over the decades ahead.

Many B&Bs—like the Water's Edge, for example—are destinations in themselves. I feel comforted to know that most of our guests are coming for a reason related to the university or the city's offerings, not because of *us*. People care about how close we are to their meeting site (which often happens to be Rackham Auditorium, across the street); they do not require an in-room fireplace or a double spa air tub.

I am glad not to be a destination. It seems to make it easier to exceed expectations. And again, if I were to express my mission as an innkeeper, it's all about exceeding expectations.

Notes to Aspiring Innkeepers

Are You Suited to Be an Innkeeper?

I know, I know. You love to cook. Everyone says you have a knack for decorating. You're a real "people person." But here are some questions to ask yourself:

- Do you tolerate all, and I mean *all,* kinds of people regardless of gender, ethnicity, sexual orientation, age, number of tattoos and tongue/eyebrow piercings, and personality quirks?

- Here's the harder question: If you have a partner, how does that partner feel about welcoming total strangers into his or her habitat? I know several couples in which person A (usually the female, but not always) is passionate about the desire to run a B&B. Spouse B is reluctant, but gives in as a gesture of love and goodwill, but then resents the intrusion and loss of privacy. Susan, a new innkeeper, promised her hesitant husband, "you don't have to interact with the guests at all," and sealed off four rooms of the house with signs marked "Private" to assure his seclusion. But he still felt invaded. So she is walking a tight wire, zealously attending to her guests, while shouldering his complaints and trying to preserve the marriage.

  If you have your heart set on opening your home to strangers and your partner is not on board, rethink the plan. Otherwise, sooner or later, your clueless guest will encounter the reluctant host and feel rebuffed. Guests can sense tension and tell if they're not entirely welcome.

- Whether you have one or more partners or are a single owner, you're going to need a relief pitcher in this 24/7 ballgame.

Fortunately, you can always hire out the pieces you can't do or don't want to do, whether it's cooking, cleaning or accounting. The cost of employing help is well worth avoiding the risk of early burnout.

- Are you comfortable with ambiguity? You're sure to sometimes hear, "I'm not sure what time we're arriving or whether or not we'll want breakfast."

- Can you handle an extremely uncertain income in the present economy?

- Are you flexible, able to instantly switch gears when someone's needs or circumstances change?

- How's your stamina? Innkeeping can be physically demanding, even if you hire out the heavy cleaning. There are still those nine grocery bags to lug up the stairs.

- Do you have a high boiling point? When things go wrong, can you blow it off or rein in your irritation? You're allowed to feel anger, but you can never, ever let anyone see you expressing it.

- How thick is your skin? Most innkeepers are people pleasers by nature, and tend to be oversensitive to other people's disappointments. That complaint posted on TripAdvisor requires two responses: first, fix the problem. Second, get over it. Which brings us to the final checkpoint:

- Rate your sense of humor. Things will go wrong, despite your best efforts. When that happens, it's imperative to lighten up. You're running a small business, not a country. It's not healthy to take ourselves too seriously.

The Top 10 Reasons
I Love Being an Innkeeper

Most people evaluate the pros and cons of becoming an innkeeper before entering the profession. But it was not until I really became immersed in the business that the benefits became clear. Early on, this list was emerging and now, fourteen years later, the rewards continue to multiply. Here, in homage to the iconic former TV host David Letterman, is my Top Ten list of reasons to be an innkeeper.

 It is 9 o'clock in the morning, and my guests have finished breakfast and are off on their day's activities. The table is cleared and the dishwasher is loaded. Most people are just beginning their work day at 9 a.m. Mine (or so I choose to pretend) has already ended.

 The dress code is slacks, shirt, and slip-on shoes. Sometimes an apron to accessorize. No more pricey designer blazer or briefcase. Since I rarely see the same people three days in a row, I can wear the same favorite comfort clothes over and over.

 There can't be a shorter commute. Our bedroom is one flight of stairs above the kitchen.

 Every day offers an excuse to use the good china; no waiting for Thanksgiving.

 Calories to burn? Cleaning and shopping constitute a good workout. Once I needed physical therapy. Now my knees are pain-free, thanks to climbing stairs off and on all day. Who needs a Stairmaster when you live in one?

Innkeeping transcends the traditional gender roles. Among innkeepers I know, men are as likely as women to do the cooking; women are as adept as any male at bookkeeping and repairs. At a state board meeting of B&B owners, I overheard three grown men discussing the merits of high thread-counts, and debating whether or not to own a mangle.

 Keeping up on world events is easy while cooking with NPR in the background. Home delivery of the *New York Times* is a reasonable business expense, not an extravagance.

 Shopping is no longer frivolous but virtuous. Cruising Amazon and eBay for best buys and bargains is a necessary pastime, not self-indulgent.

 Whatever you have to buy—from printer cartridges to pillow shams—is tax deductible.

 And the number one reason for being an innkeeper is of course … the people! Consistently interesting and appreciative, they enrich our lives. Some folks get to travel the world. When you're an innkeeper, the world comes to you.

…. And the One Reason Not To

The money.

None of the how-to books promise that running a B&B will make you a fortune. No innkeeper in my acquaintance is a one-percenter. A B&B with four or fewer guestrooms is better looked upon as a hobby than a high income source. A larger, busier inn brings in more revenue but costs more to run.

Focus instead on the intrinsic rewards, which include independence, self-employment, living in beautiful surroundings, and sharing them with some of the most interesting people you might ever encounter.

FIVE

Out With The Old

For two people who had spent early careers in separate orbits, Bob and I proved surprisingly compatible in running the B&B together. I like being up with the birds and setting out breakfast; he doesn't mind waiting for a guest who's arriving at 11:00 p.m. He's the computer whiz, so he was best suited to choose and master the PC-based reservation systems. And as Mr. Infrastructure, he researched and replaced the behemoth 40-year-old furnace that literally filled half of the basement and sounded like an emerging tanker truck. The furnace decision did not need my input, as my aptitude is more along the lines of shopping for placemats.

I focused like a laser on the aesthetic aspects of developing the B&B—the fun part, as I saw it. We had purchased the B&B "turnkey," which means that everything we needed to run the business, from beds and dressers to sheets and saucers, were included as part of the sale. But on closer look, the towels were thin, the dishes were dingy, and the furniture not to my liking. Floral prints abounded. For example, one of the smaller rooms had white-painted furniture, a fuchsia carpet, and a ruffled bedspread with pink-and-green cabbage roses along with matching tie-back curtains. The look was straight from the pages of *American Girl* magazine. And it seemed to me that every third person checking into that room was a burly male nearly seven-feet tall.

So we donated the bed and its flower-patterned bedding to the Kiwanis Thrift Sale, and carried the ungainly mahogany buffet and six-foot wide vanity dresser to the front lawn. (Overnight guests do not need fourteen drawers of clothing space.) On a warm October Saturday, we had created an outdoor furniture showcase with pieces priced to sell. Those items that remained by noon were tagged "make an offer." And finally, the stragglers were "free to a good home."

I was left with some petty cash and an empty canvas.

We brought over a few family pieces from the 1842 farmhouse where we'd raised our kids, and which we still owned across town. It was currently being rented to a visiting professor and his family on sabbatical at the University of Michigan. To create space for their belongings, we'd put some of our furniture and most of our personal paraphernalia—family photos and the like—in storage. So in 2003, I already had a fair number of items to feather our new nest. The gaps could be filled via Ann Arbor's consignment stores, craigslist, and the infinite global marketplace of Amazon.com.

Open During Construction

While I was comparison shopping for throw rugs, Bob was buying lumber at Lowe's.

He has always been more visionary. I open a walk-in closet and see a space to hang clothes. He sees potential for a tiled bathroom with dual pedestal sinks and a soaking tub. I look at a wall and wonder which picture to hang on it. Bob thinks about moving the wall.

Our son Marc was his willing accomplice. Since more rooms would equal more revenue, we'd decided to convert the two remaining two-room apartments into four separate guestrooms. Marc, who ran his own painting/remodeling business, installed modern-tiled bathrooms within the ample living rooms of the apartments. The bedroom wings already had en suite bathrooms, so they were ready to rent without further embellishment.

With up to three or four walls making up each individual bedroom, bathroom and hallway, the B&B had more than one hundred white walls. Not the warm appealing cozy white of new-fallen snow, but the institutional chalk white you might find in a county lock-up facility. If those walls could talk they'd have cried out, "Please! Color me!" And Marc was never timid about color. He'd start with a bright neutral (Wyndham Cream was a favorite) but then he'd make it pop with an accent wall of forest green or sunset orange. There was no beige on his palette.

We gave each of the rooms a theme based on places we like: Charleston (South Carolina) the city where I grew up; Maine Woods celebrates a state we have come to love, discovered with friends who live there. Room themes make decorating fun but a little more limiting. You can't hang the print of Monet's *Water Lilies* next to the moose-base lamp in Maine Woods. Gifts that my housekeeper Martha had brought from her native Kenya also posed a challenge. I could hardly place the carved wooden giraffe in the Maine Woods or Charleston rooms.

Consequently, we named our ninth guestroom Jamboree, a word that sounds lively, exuberant, and unrestricted. Jamboree was a room we could decorate any way we wanted, from orchids to elephants.

Using layers of aquamarine and crystal foam, Marc faux painted the arched ceiling over the bed in the Laguna Beach room to resemble a crashing wave. He nailed half logs to the walls of the Yellowstone room, turning it into the cozy inside of a little log cabin. Each of our rooms has its own radiant personality: The Boston Freedom Trail room has an eighteenth-century air with a Queen Anne–style headboard and wingback chairs. Maine Woods is more rustic, like Yellowstone, with yellow-pine furniture and moose silhouettes on the lamp shades. And finally, having let go of the dream of owning a B&B on a beach, we compensated by giving the two ground-floor guestrooms a beach theme, naming them Sandcastle and Ocean View. A surprising number of callers (most of them from the West Coast) take these names quite literally, saying to us, "I didn't realize Ann Arbor was on the ocean!"

Throughout fall 2003 and well into 2004, half of our rooms were under construction. There was never a question of closing for the duration; we needed the revenue to pay for the remodeling. And here's the thing we found about B&B guests; they never conveyed the least sense of inconvenience. Unfailingly good natured and go-with-the-flow, they gamely stepped over the two by fours and inched past a drywall sheet as if it were nothing more than a vertical welcome mat. "You're doing some renovations?" they would say. "Good for you! Can't wait to return and see the results."

By 2004, the sawdust had settled and our nine rooms, each with its own en-suite bathroom, were fully operational. But the upcycling of furniture and accessories continued through the years ahead. A serviceable wooden rocker was replaced by a more comfortable cushiony armchair; a queen bed was swapped for a pillow-top king. The nineteen-inch televisions were upgraded to thirty-six-inch models, each of them covering the top of their respective dressers. Within ten years, they too were outdated, and replaced by wall-mounted flat-screen TVs.

The B&B would always be a work in progress.

In Search of Style

Thrust into the entrepreneurial world of business ownership, I joined the Ann Arbor Chamber of Commerce. I couldn't make the 7:00 a.m. Tuesday breakfast meetings (B&Bs are generally a little busy at that hour) but I decided to try the monthly "Lunch and Learn." It was a chance to dress up for a change and, as they say, "network."

The luncheon took place in the large conference room of the local Marriott. After a predictable chicken salad and a speaker who read to us aloud from her PowerPoint slides, it was time for member introductions. We were to go around the room, table by table, and each stand and give a ten-second marketing pitch. "Hi. I'm Pat Materka and I own the Ann Arbor Bed and Breakfast. We have nine rooms, each with private baths, Wi-Fi, and on-site parking. We're located at Huron and Fletcher, right across from the U-of-M Central Campus."

There. Exactly ten seconds.

I should not have been surprised when a smartly suited young woman swooped down on me as soon as the meeting ended. She was wearing a black-pencil skirt, hounds-tooth checked jacket, and a nametag identifying her as an interior designer. "I would *love* to come over to see your place!"

Mavis said eagerly, extending her business card. "Maybe I could offer you some suggestions? I wouldn't charge you anything, of course."

As I mentioned, we'd spent the past thirty years in an 1842 farmhouse. It had pine-plank floors and rustic post-and-beam construction, giving it the ambiance of a weathered country barn missing its hayloft. From my antiques foraging, I'd filled the rooms with "primitives," like dry sinks and sap buckets. With no false modesty, I can say that I'd mastered the "country" look.

But to be honest, Mid-Century Modern had me stumped. I didn't know what to put in the sunken living room, but I knew it couldn't be a butter churn.

So to Mavis, the certified interior designer, I said, "Sure, how about this Thursday?" I had heard that professionals like her have access to big discounts at designer showrooms, ones that are off-limits to the rest of us mortals. Her beguiling sales pitch was irresistible: the more you spend, the more you save.

Mavis appeared two days later, brimming with enthusiasm. She swept through each of the bedrooms, gushing over their potential. "Let me come back next week with some furniture catalogs and fabric samples," she offered. Would I mind writing her a $75 check to cover her time and costs?

Fair enough. I turned over the first of what became a series of $75 consulting fees. Six weeks later, we were still poring through photographs. I began to sense that even if Mavis had access to furniture at a wholesale rate, her markup would make it equivalent to retail. One afternoon she arrived carrying a rolled-up twelve-foot oriental carpet runner and unfurled it across the slate floor. It could be mine for $1,400.

Mavis seemed dedicated and competent, and I admired her gumption. But I did not, it was turning out, admire her taste. It's not that she didn't have *good* taste; it just wasn't my taste. Whatever that was.

I realized this is the same reason I've puzzled over people who hire personal shoppers. Why give up the fun of perusing the sales rack by paying someone else to select your wardrobe? I was reminded of number three on my Top Ten list of reasons for being an innkeeper:

Shopping is no longer frivolous but virtuous. Cruising Amazon and eBay for best buys and bargains is a necessary pastime, not self-indulgent.

So Mavis and I parted ways. The B&B was our home, after all, and it needed to be a reflection of "us," not a designer's interpretation of "us." The room furnishings would evolve at their own pace. The only piece of furniture that guests really cared about, I recognized, was the one they'd be sleeping on.

Threads in Shreds

The mattresses were decent, although over the next five years we would come to replace each of the with top-of-the-line pillow-tops. But the sheets and towels I inherited from the previous owner were another matter. They were so frayed and thin they were almost translucent. No yard sale for them; they could only be donated. We bundled them up for the Humane Society of Huron Valley, which we had learned is always happy to accept sheets and towels. Puppies are not fussy about thread counts.

Speaking of which, higher is not necessarily better. I've learned that very high-thread counts are actually woven from thinner split fibers. They may feel soft, but after going through the dryer, they become wrinkled as raisins. In my experience, 300-thread counts hold up better than 1,200 and are more readily affordable at the discount malls I favor. When you set out to replace up to thirty sets of sheets, it pays to shop T.J. Maxx, not Neiman Marcus.

A happy homemaking manual I was given years ago—it was probably a hint from my mother—advised that one should own three sets of sheets for each bed: one set to use, one to launder, and a third to "rest" on the shelf. Apparently the cotton fibers need to relax in the closet (who knew?) before being returned to the bed.

There was no R&R for our sheets and pillowcases, however. On days that we were turning over all nine rooms, the sheets went full circle from the bed into the washer, to the dryer, and then back on the mattress. Actually, this still seems more efficient because it eliminates the tedious step of folding and stacking the sheets in the linen closets.

An aside: How is it that my housekeepers can fold fitted sheets into perfect origami rectangles, while my efforts resemble a wadded-up newspaper? I never did master the process, though I've learned how to do something much more important:

Delegate.

You'll find more on that handy practice in Chapter 10, entitled "Help!"

Once I'd cracked the code surrounding thread counts, it seemed a simple matter to purchase the sheets. How could anyone get that wrong? Here's how: buy multiple sets in exactly the same pattern and color. I was so taken by Ralph Lauren's cobalt-blue-and-white paisley pattern—a steal at fifty percent off—I bought multiple sets in king, queen, and twin sizes. What was I thinking? Stacked in the linen closet, each folded sheet looked exactly the same. It was impossible to tell one size from another. I soon learned that if I were hurrying to change over a bed for a last-minute check-in, the first sheets I grabbed for a king bed would fit a queen. Every time.

Solution

Eliminate confusion by color-coding your sheets by size; e.g., green for king, yellow for queen, and so on. What could be simpler?

That said, many innkeepers favor buying all linens in white, since stains and shoe-scuff marks (do guests jump up and down on the beds?) can be treated with bleach. You simply need to designate different shelves for different sizes. To me, white seemed bland, boring, and hotel-like. I wanted to show guests that a B&B, at least *my* B&B, is different from a traditional hotel. But there was a downside. Some skin-care products apparently contain an ingredient that bleaches towels and pillowcases on contact. Green, for example, turns sunburst yellow. A pair of new fluffy, lime-green bath towels emerged from the laundry with yellow splotches that resembled a Rorschach inkblot test. Alas, stains on white towels can be bleached away, but bleach stains on colored towels are there to stay. These towels too were donated to the Humane Society to line puppy crates.

Call it the cost of doing business. Dishes break, milk spills, and sometimes the sheet or towel I bought only the week before is rendered unusable. Get over it. It's a nuisance, not a catastrophe. In those early days of the B&B, when there was not enough time to wash and dry towels before the next check-in, I simply dashed off to HomeGoods and bought new ones to replace them. All I had to do was snip off the price tags.

That's how I learned that it's prudent to run new towels through the washer and dryer before putting them out for use. This was especially true of the deep colors I favored at the beginning. "The navy blue towels in our bathroom must be brand-new," guessed a good-humored guest when she came up for breakfast. Smiling, she showed me her bare arm. It was clean, dry, and colorfully flecked with navy-blue lint.

SIX

Décor and More

I may have been stymied by the sunken living room, but I knew exactly how to fill the shelves overlooking the dining room. They were perfect for displaying my collection of antique toys.

For some twenty-five years, I'd rented a booth at the monthly Ann Arbor Antiques Market. Buying and selling and buying and selling yielded a small profit, most of which was invested in—you guessed it—yet more antiques. We antique lovers put up with selling only to support our true passion: buying.

At first I specialized in country furniture and accessories, like pine drop-leaf tables, steamer trunks, apple crates, and the like. Then I noticed that the toy versions of these items often sold for more than their full-sized counterparts. Why lug a seven-foot Hoosier cabinet to the market when a four-teen-inch miniature version weighed under a pound and yielded a higher profit margin?

That is, if I actually were to sell it. Inevitably, buying gives way to keeping. I greedily hung onto my favorites, like the tin chicken that laid marbles when a lever is pushed, and the Brownie Hawkeye flash camera identical to the one I owned at age ten. Some people love crystal and fine china. I'm drawn to toys from my 1950s childhood.

Those items were just waiting to live in a bed and breakfast. If you are an innkeeper, the odds are that you are a collector. Like cooking and catering, collecting seems to be part of our genetic makeup.

In fact, for many of us innkeepers, one of the most appealing aspects of running a B&B is that it provides an excuse to show off our beloved *stuff*. What is the point of owning without sharing? Across one wall of our sunny south-facing dining room, my son Marc built three panels of display shelves of varying heights and depths. On these I lined up my Hopalong Cassidy lunchbox, miniature Singer sewing machine, and assorted tin wind-up toys. "I remember playing with one of those when I was a child!" is a comment I hear regularly. Or, "Wow, these sure bring back memories."

However, there's one incident involving the toy shelf that stands out among the rest.

Early in our tenure as innkeepers, we hosted a New York writer on a book tour, along with his socialite wife. He had given a reading and book-signing at one of our local bookstores. It was still dark outside when I served them a 6:00 a.m. breakfast before their return to the airport for an early flight. The author's literary agent arranged their stay with us, and I sensed from their bearing that they were more accustomed to the Four Seasons than a homey B&B.

Still, they tried to be gracious. Sleepily noticing my collection of antique toys lined up on the shelves, the wife asked politely, "So are you operating a childcare center during the day, as well as a bed and breakfast?"

Lose the Tchotchkes

The toys may be my most colorful collection but they are hardly the only one. There's a grouping of family photographs; an inevitable assortment of B&B recipe books; and a sleigh of stuffed penguins greeting guests at the entrance. My decorating style, if you can call it a style, has been called "whimsical" and "eclectic" but it has never been described as "minimalist."

It's tempting to adorn every surface from bureau to bedstead. But now, as we outfitted each guestroom, I trained myself to ask: is this item necessary or is it clutter? Will this add to the guest experience or get in the way?

The guests themselves have taught me restraint. Here's what I heard from men: "What I don't like about some B&Bs is that there are so many doodads on the dressers and desks, I have no place to put my stuff." One fellow described a Victorian-era inn in which every chest had a lace doily, and atop every doily stood a vase of dried flowers and a china figurine. There was no space for his toiletries on the pedestal sink.

And the women wonder: "How do you keep it all dusted?"

If you're driven to decorate, do it with things that hang or attach on the wall. Pictures, mirrors, sconces, decorative light-switch covers, and nightlights add ambiance without taking up space. And heed this advice:

"I'll tell you what this room needs," growled one of my early guests, a middle-aged male passing through Ann Arbor. "Hooks!

"I'm the type of guy who'd rather toss my pants on a hook overnight than take time to fool around with a hanger." Quick as a jackrabbit, I drove over to Ace Hardware. By afternoon there were sturdy chrome hooks installed on the inside walls of every closet and on the backs of all available doors.

Lesson: Solicit and welcome complaints. Each one is an opportunity for improvement.

B&B guests are not very demanding, but there are three things they're counting on:

* a comfortable bed,
* a private bathroom, and
* a clear space and surfaces for their belongings.

"Keep it simple" refers to the bed as well as the bureau, a lesson I've also learned from guests. Sleek is better than stuffy. You *can* have too many throw pillows.

Notes to Aspiring Innkeepers

Express Yourself

You may favor flocked wallpaper or those chandeliers made from moose horns. Room decorating is one of the more enjoyable perks of innkeeping. Since we cannot possibly know our guests' style preferences, we get to follow our own instincts. Conservative or flamboyant: it's our call.

People seek out B&Bs for the very reason that each of our inns is different. Traditional hotel rooms are predictable and neutral. Think "B" words: beige, bland, and boring. B&Bs are all about "E" words, like eclectic and even eccentric. Let your inn reflect who you are.

Of course, you'll clear the guest rooms of personal memorabilia. Your 30-year-old son's vacated bedroom-turned-guestroom cannot display his high school hockey trophies. It's no longer a shrine. But do let the common areas reflect your hobbies and your interests. And don't resist showing photos of your parents and children. Many B&B guests *want* to know their hosts on a more personal level, and photos are great conversation starters.

As you outfit the optimal guestroom, here are some key considerations:

- Make room for a bedside table and reading lamp on *each side* of the bed.

- Accommodate differences in sleeping preferences by layering the bed covering: a light blanket followed by a heavier comforter, bedspread, or quilt. Offer both firm pillows and softer squishy ones.

- Keep in mind that some guests are allergic to down, so if you offer this luxury, have alternative pillows or coverings with synthetic filling.

- If you're carpeting the bedrooms, choose a durable short tight pile, such as Berber or a tweed. Long fluffy fibers feel good on your bare toes but also show footprints, as I discovered through trial and repeated error. The solution was a rug rake. But really, do you want to spend the valuable time of your life raking a rug?

SEVEN

Curb Appeal

You don't have to be a gardener to run a B&B. But I think you have to have a garden. Or at least, a pot of geraniums flanking the front entrance.

Our building covers most of its property line, with a large parking lot filling nearly every inch of the side and the rear. Banked along the front of the building was a row of cone-shaped arborvitae, and in front of them, a short swath of lawn reaching out to the sidewalk. Over the next ten years, we replaced the scraggly arborvitae with colorful perennials along with sunflowers and an array of annuals. It's always a work in progress. As the saying goes, "a garden is never as great as it's going to be *next* year."

A garden needn't be large to have an impact, nor does it need to be labor intensive. If weeding and deadheading aren't your idea of bliss, hire it out. It's well worth the investment.

Landscape and flowers are as integral to the B&B ambiance as mattresses and pillows. Your well-kept lawn welcomes guests before they even enter the driveway. An attractive landscape is both an amenity and a marketing tool. A realtor would call it "curb appeal." It's a marquee announcing, "Hey, if you think this looks nice on the outside, wait until you see the inside!"

A garden is also a gift to your neighbors and others who pass it. One of our most touching experiences was a postcard we received, addressed only to "B&B Owners." It read:

"Your very beautiful front gardens have brightened and lightened our frequent trips past your home to the University Hospital. Thought you would like to know that even strangers appreciate your hard work. We look upon the gardens as our living 'get-well card'."

EIGHT

Extreme Shopping

Some people decompress after a long day at work by running five miles. Others sink into a hot tub or channel surf with a bowl of chips and a beer.

I go shopping.

Shopping, for me, is not just a way to unwind; it's a way to rev up. Any time, any place. In the lifetime before I became an innkeeper, you could find me cruising a weekend antiques market at 5:00 a.m., just as the dealers were unloading their wares. On other weekends, I'd head for the neighborhood yard sales or holiday craft bazaars. I've stood in line for the door-buster specials on Black Friday, and heard weary store clerks lock the doors behind me at the close of Midnight Madness. It's never too early in the morning nor too late at night to go shopping.

I should clarify that shopping does not necessarily mean *buying*. Buying can be an expensive habit that can burden your life with a lot of unnecessary stuff. Recreational shopping engages the imagination; it's low-impact aerobic exercise. Using a pedometer, you'll find out that you can log in a mile or two walking the periphery of a typical shopping mall. A department store is a museum in which all of the exhibits happen to be for sale. It costs nothing to check out the clearance racks at Macy's. There's no admission fee for this mindless entertainment, and no minimum purchase is required.

I'm not ashamed to enjoy shopping, but I'm not inclined to boast about it. It's acceptable, even admirable, to be a fanatic about hiking, biking, or baking. But shopping? It sounds so flighty and irresponsible.

So imagine my delight to be part of a profession that not only condones shopping, but demands it. No longer a guilty pleasure, shopping is as essential to running a bed and breakfast as, well, making beds and making breakfasts. Citing again one of my Top Ten Reasons for Becoming an Innkeeper:

 Shopping is no longer frivolous but virtuous. Cruising Amazon (the website, not the river) and eBay for best buys and bargains is an essential part of the business, not an empty pastime.

In the heady weeks and months after we bought the inn, I was in my element. Every room needed something, and some rooms needed everything. Our bookings were vigorous from the start, with all nine rooms filled on many weekends. On busy mornings, the washer and dryer could not keep pace with the turnovers. If a room was to have fresh sheets before three o'clock check-in, I absolutely had to go out and buy a new set of sheets. My car beat a well-worn path to T.J. Maxx and HomeGoods.

Bed linens weren't the only urgent need in those early days. On one occasion, it was the bed itself. A couple visiting the campus forgot to mention they were bringing their teenage daughter. Oops! Off to Mattress City to buy a rollaway. Ultimately, we acquired four stow-away single bed frames and mattresses so that we could accommodate as many extra people as the inn could hold.

Finally, there comes a point when you survey the surroundings and declare "enough." The linen closet is stocked; the kitchen is equipped; and every room has the requisite desk and chair, twin bedside tables, lamps and alarm clock. The nest is feathered.

And yet, furnished does not mean you're finished.

There's still the never-ending matter of groceries.

To Market, To Market

Here lies the exception to the shopping-doesn't-mean-spending rule. Who goes to the supermarket just to *view* the produce? I'm there to buy, not browse. So perhaps this is the chapter in which you expect to read expert advice on how to save time and money on groceries; how to serve twenty for breakfast with economy and flair.

You won't find it here.

It's no surprise that next to the mortgage, food is the largest expense on our spreadsheet. While I try to be cost-conscious (bypassing, for example, imported blueberries in January), we're extravagant by most standards. It goes back to the decision to serve breakfast as a buffet instead of apportioned on plates. A lavish buffet, especially on leisurely weekends, compels guests to take second and third helpings. And once you've set the bar at fresh-squeezed orange juice, there's no going back to frozen concentrate.

Anyway, cost isn't the issue. I don't mind spending hundreds of dollars each week buying groceries. But I'm appalled by the hundreds of hours it takes to do it.

Counting the quick stops at the bakery and major expeditions to Costco, I average ten to fifteen hours a week shopping, shuttling, and shelving groceries. That works out to seven hundred hours a year or more than one month of my waking life. Every day, we seem to run out of something essential. The egg carton that I blithely assumed was full when I glanced in the refrigerator? Turns out, it contains one egg, not a dozen. If I'm lucky, I'll discover this *after* all of my guests have eaten and not midway through breakfast. Regardless, it sends me back to the supermarket. These excursions are as much a part of my daily routine as eating and sleeping. And it's not just food items, but other staples, like soap, tissues, and trash bags. If I get overconfident and skip a day, you can bet that I'll discover we're out of laundry detergent on a Sunday with nine turnovers.

This is embarrassing, because back in the 80s, I wrote a book on time management, with a riveting chapter on expedient shopping. The message was simple:

- Plan ahead;
- Make a list;
- Actually take the list with you to the store;

- Stockpile the staples (bread, juice, yogurt, eggs), obsessively checking expiration dates; and
- Choose fruits and vegetables with attention to flavor, freshness and shelf life. Broccoli might keep over a week in the refrigerator; pineapple and melon, several days. Those fragile raspberries need to be enjoyed within a day of their purchase.

And yet even after fourteen years as an innkeeper, it happens. At 7:00 a.m. I open the refrigerator to find we are way short on milk, a beverage for which there is no viable substitute. "Sorry we're out of milk. Would you care for some orange juice on your corn flakes this morning?"

Let me end on the same positive note that began this chapter. I like shopping, and don't begrudge the time it takes. Even the boring, banal trip through the supermarket aisles with its attendant rituals, like checking the cartons for cracked eggs and inspecting the bottom of the berry container for mold, can be approached with a spirit of adventure and capped by a sense of accomplishment.

Watching the food as it rolls down the conveyor belt and into my plastic recycle tote bags, I'm reminded of my favorite children's book by Watty Piper. I've become *The Little Engine That Could,* bringing all the bright red-cheeked apples and golden juicy oranges to the good little boys and girls who live on the other side of the mountain. They're spending the night at my inn.

I think I can—I think I can—I think I can.

If nothing else, the supermarket offers a break from the computer screen where I spend way too many sedentary hours. It holds the promise of finding some unexpected dinner treat in the bakery section, and the rare opportunity to read *The National Enquirer* in the checkout line and find out the latest on the outsized lives of Brad, Angelina, and Jennifer.

NINE

Coming Clean

The summer after I graduated from high school, my mother gave me an ultimatum: "Either you find a summer job," she announced cheerily over dinner, "or I can teach you how to do housework."

Housework? This wasn't an opportunity. It was a threat. "I'm getting a job," I promised, and within a week, I found a position in sales and marketing.

Or to be more precise, I became a door-to-door salesperson. Dressed in my best school clothes and carrying an authoritative clipboard, I canvassed the local subdivisions. My employer was *The West Ashley Journal*, a new weekly newspaper in Charleston, South Carolina, aiming to build readership. I wore out two pairs of sandals as I crossed lawns, rang doorbells and offered my spiel, filling out forms in triplicate. I received a one-dollar commission for each subscription sold.

I didn't earn six figures that summer. I'm not even sure I managed to earn three figures by the time I left for college in September. But that summer job got me out of the house, and more important, it got me out of the housework.

Missing my mother's course in Cleaning 101 was no cause for regret. Through the early years of marriage, housework was so far down on my list of priorities, you'd have to dig a hole to uncover it. As the comedienne Phyllis Diller put it:

Cleaning your house while your kids are still growing
is like shoveling the walk before it stops snowing.

I saw clutter as an inevitable consequence of creativity, and doesn't everyone view creativity as something positive? You've heard the saying, "A clean desk is a sign of an empty mind." I framed it over my desk in needlepoint.

As a family, we lowered our standards. My children understood that if a newspaper left on the couch offended them, they could certainly remove it. If a room was messy, close the door. As for making the bed, well, what was the point if you were only going to crawl back into it sixteen hours later and muss it up again? "There is no such thing as an unmade bed," I proclaimed. "The bed is being *aired.*"

You get the picture. Page back to chapter four, which closed with a list of character traits under the heading, "Are you suited to be an innkeeper?" If "neat" had been a requirement, I'd never have made the cut.

But this carefree attitude won't fly when you're running a B&B. You can outfit the guestrooms in museum-quality King Louis XIV bureaus and headboards, and it will not impress if there's even a speck of dust apparent. Every surface has to gleam and shine.

It's been said that people can't change—but I changed. Since becoming an innkeeper, I've changed sheets, furnace filters, and batteries in smoke alarms. I've also changed my mind. Cleaning doesn't have to be drudgery; it can even be energizing. And clutter is not a sign of creativity; in fact, it's a deterrent. In a clean, clear environment you can get far more accomplished.

In Pursuit of Spotless

Cleaning a bed and breakfast turned out to be no different from cleaning any other typical ten-bedroom, twelve-bathroom family home, except that the bar is set much higher. Innkeepers cannot simply meet their own housekeeping standards (which in my case were low to middling). We must anticipate and exceed our guests' standards, which can be sky high.

There are two stages of B&B housekeeping service: *refresh* and *turnover.*

Refresh is for guests who are staying over. This includes remaking the beds, emptying the wastebaskets, removing empty soda cans and used coffee cups, and tidying the bathroom. I eschewed the preachy signs that hotels post about conserving water and saving the environment. We know that a damp towel left on the bathroom floor is code for "please exchange this for a fresh one."

A *turnover* happens after the guests check out and the room is restored to its pristine condition. We change the sheets, scour the bathroom, change out the used towels and bath rugs, wipe down every surface, vacuum the carpet, dust the blinds, and so on.

It's been a revelation to observe the contrasts in people's sleep patterns. Some guests take up less than a quarter of a king-size bed. They appear to curl up like field mice in the upper corner near the alarm clock. The rest of the bed lies smooth and undisturbed, with even the pillows and shams in place. Remaking this bed for a stayover takes all of ten seconds. Laundering the sheets after the guest leaves feels wasteful (though mandatory), since 80 percent of the bedding has never been never touched human skin.

At the opposite extreme is the thrasher. Pillows are punched and flung, blankets askew, sheets twisted into ropes and knots. The bed looks like it's been through a Mixmaster. Remaking a bed in this condition can take longer than changing it. You have to wonder what it's like to sleep with a thrasher, if one is able to sleep at all.

Where Credit is Due

I notice I used the word "we" throughout my discussion of tidying and turn-overs. That is misleading. The truth is, I'm blessed with a team of part-time housekeepers who handle nearly all of the B&B cleaning and laundry without the need for my input or oversight. Their dedication and skill is unmatched. Incredibly, these women never call in sick, and on the rare day that one of them cannot be here, she arranges for one of her coworkers to substitute. The system works seamlessly.

Except when it doesn't.

Every so often a room gets missed or is intentionally left to be cleaned the following day. Then suddenly it turns out that the unready room is needed after all. A guest is coming at 6:00 p.m. and we must resort to the ancillary backup crew. That would be me.

Let me tell you, I am grateful to my housekeepers every day that they're here. But I appreciate them even more profoundly when they are *not* here. That's when I realize how physically hard these women work, wielding armloads of wet laundry from washer to dryer, moving furniture to wipe down baseboards, kneeling on the cold hard tile to scour tubs.

I don't mind making beds. Watching the crisp clean sheets billow like parachutes onto the mattress, folding the top sheet evenly over the blanket, and arranging the pillows symmetrically is sensuous and satisfying. Making a bed is like wrapping a gift.

It's while cleaning the bathroom that my spirits sink. Globs of toothpaste and soap scum in the sink set me to wondering *Why am I doing this? Why did I become an innkeeper?* Living alone looks mighty appealing. But the mood never lasts. All in all, I still love running a B&B, and on some days, cleaning toilets is part of the package.

But then there's the hair. Long curly filaments of human hair clinging to the shower and sink in undulating S's and curlicues, impossible to grasp with my fingers. Nor do stray hairs adhere to a wet paper towel. And the more I look, the more I find. This person sheds like a border collie. Finally, I rise from my knees and drag the canister vacuum cleaner into the bathroom. It's a clumsy appliance, but its powerful hose attachment sucks up the hair and at last, the porcelain is clear and sparkling.

Cleaning a bathroom always conjures up my vision of the Perfect Guest. You may think I'm referring to charisma and warmth—a person who is friendly, considerate, and kind. But my perfect guest is characterized by appearance, not personality traits.

He—or she—is hairless as a newborn infant, clean-shaven, and bald as an egg.

Cleaning 101: A Crib Sheet

It's too late for me to learn Mandarin or take up the violin, but it's never too late to collect those cleaning tips I missed in high school. Here are a few winners:

- Don't lug cleaning supplies from bathroom to bathroom. Store everything you need—cleaners, paper towels, sponges, scrub brushes—in the cabinet under the sink. Unless it's a pedestal sink, in which case, stash them in a nearby closet.

- Purchase a number of empty spray bottles from the dollar store and fill with a solution of 50 percent water and 50 percent distilled white vinegar for a cheap and highly effective all-purpose glass and tile cleaner.

- Use old newspapers (if you can find any that are still being published) to clean windows and mirrors, lint-free. Coffee filters serve this purpose as well.

- Never throw out a toothbrush. They're perfect for cleaning grit from crevices that sponges can't penetrate.

- Treat a stain (on a napkin, for example) as soon as you see it before tossing it into the laundry pile, instead of waiting to inspect it prior to washing.

- Finally, I admire spiders, those ingenious architects of the insect world, but realize most guests do not look upon webs as artwork. A bough of eucalyptus in well-placed corners will repel spiders without harming them and induce them to move outdoors for their construction projects.

Notes to Aspiring Innkeepers

Refreshing a room for stayovers is standard procedure for hotels, but not necessarily all B&Bs. Each of us determines our own level of service. Most of the innkeepers I know tidy rooms on a daily basis, including changing the sheets every three to four days during a long-term stay.

But one states his policy as follows:

"Out of respect for your privacy, we will not enter your room during your stay. Please let us know if you need fresh linens or other amenities."

This is a clever way to appear incredibly considerate while reducing your workload.

Some guests are compulsive about making their beds themselves; others instruct us not to bother. We provide "Do Not Disturb" doorknob hangers and will not enter or service a room that displays one.

But Chris Mason, who owns the Parish House Inn in Ypsilanti, Michigan, has a different viewpoint. "It's my home and I have the right to check each room daily," she insists, speaking from twenty-plus years of experience. "You never know whether something is going on, such as smoking, which could have damaging consequences."

TEN

Help!

I grew up in a 900-square-foot, three-bedroom tract home—typical for the 1950s and tiny by today's standards. The 1842 farmhouse in which we raised our kids was not much larger before we built an addition, and even then it remained modest. So taking on a 6000-square-foot behemoth was no minor adjustment.

But the size of the B&B was not intimidating. It was the fact that in order to handle it, I'd have to hire help.

Now, plenty of people would welcome this challenge. I've had colleagues who measured their status by the number of underlings who report to them. "I've just been made head of marketing," a friend in the pharmaceutical industry announced happily. "I'll oversee forty-five salespeople!"

Was I jealous? No way. Her triumph was my nightmare. During all my years at the University of Michigan, I'd never even managed an intern, and that was by choice. In each of my overlapping career paths, as a newspaper reporter, antique dealer, event planner, adjunct instructor, I worked independently. I'd never *wanted* to supervise staff or subordinates. I worked hard to raise two responsible children so I did not have to supervise *them*.

Nor did I ever want to employ a housekeeper. I could not imagine asking, even if I was paying, someone to do chores I disliked doing myself. Instead, we just lowered our hygiene standards and lived with a layer of clutter. On the occasions I *did* haul out the vacuum cleaner, no doubt due to an impending visit from my in-laws, I called it aerobics. I congratulated myself for saving money twice: first, by not having to pay a cleaning service, and second, for getting exercise without joining a gym.

That strategy worked fine for our family home, where you could dim lights and close doors, but not if you're running a business. A bed and breakfast is like a house that is always on the market, with a perpetual "For Sale" sign on the lawn. Every room must be neat, pristine, and ready for inspection. I had neither the aptitude nor ambition to maintain this extreme level of spotlessness.

Worse, I foresaw weekends when we could expect all rooms to be occupied, which meant nine full turnovers on an average Sunday. If each room took an hour apiece to clean…, well, you do the math. I obviously needed someone to help me.

I needed Cleopatra.

Beginner's Training

With her buoyant personality and constant smile, Cleo was as charming as her Egyptian namesake. "I am learning so much from you," she kept saying, and I was beguiled by the flattery. I was also impressed by her backstory. At age twenty, Cleo had come to the U.S. from Africa on a student visa. What made her choose Ann Arbor? "Because all over Kenya I saw people wearing yellow-and-blue University of Michigan T-shirts," she explained. "Michigan was the only place I'd heard of in America."

At the time that we bought the B&B, Cleo had been working for Edith, the previous owner, for nearly a year. That seemed promising. Keeping her on would save me the ordeal of advertising, interviewing, and hiring. I was told that Cleo was eager to keep her job and hey, she had experience!

Edith did not exactly offer a ringing endorsement. "You need check her work very carefully," she warned ominously, her eyes narrowing. But Cleo gave me no qualms. "Oh thank you, thank you, thank you!" she gushed when I called her to extend the job offer. "I would love to keep working at the

B&B! This is my dream come true!" Her eagerness won me over. Enthusiasm and gratitude: what more could I ask for?

I would soon learn the answer: dedication and competence.

Cleo, my first employee ever, and I became a team. Her job was to clean the rooms. My job was to re-clean them and fix her mistakes. I followed behind her like a devoted puppy. She was the engine; I the caboose. With Cleo, there was sure to be an un-emptied wastebasket or a damp sliver of soap left in the shower stall. It never crossed my mind to reprimand her or insist she be more conscientious. I just quietly covered her oversights, thanking her profusely for her efforts.

Cleo would not have lasted long at the Ritz-Carlton. Or for that matter, at Motel 6.

But what did I know? I had never had an employee. I was drawn to her cheery disposition and made allowances for her youth. I felt maternal towards Cleopatra, and like many a mother, I was blind to her flaws. My conversations with Cleo seemed to consist of "Great job!" (even when it clearly wasn't), and "Thanks for coming in!"

> Cleo had a talent for changing her hairdo- straightened and sleek one week, braided in cornrows the next.
> One morning she arrived with a cascade of ringlets. "Cleo, I didn't realize your hair was so long," I remarked naively, having never heard of such a thing as hair extensions. "Oh Pat," she replied fondly, "you're so white."

Raising the Bar

A nine-guestroom B&B needed more than a part-time helper and me. Within a year, I hired Martha, whose polish and professionalism was a welcome contrast to Cleo's carelessness. At thirty-five, she was a few years older than Cleo but decades more mature. Martha also grew up in Kenya where she had worked in the hotel industry. "I have missed being in this environment," she said with a smile, embracing her new assignment with gusto.

Martha had joined her husband Ali in America shortly before giving birth to their daughter Shamim (which means "beloved" in Swahili) on January 1, 2000. I felt an immediate bond with this millennium baby and her brother Jay, who was a month old when I hired Martha. With her commitment and work ethic, Martha raised the housekeeping standards at the B&B to a five-star level.

Which created a problem. In fact, a crisis.

Cleo continued her lackadaisical ways. With Martha on board, I began to relax about checking and re-checking the rooms, knowing my new house-keeper would cover all bases. Over the months that followed, I did not realize the extent to which Martha was covering for Cleo's negligence. One week-end when Bob and I were away and a friend was filling in to serve breakfast, Martha came by in the evening to assess the next day's work. On top of the dryer, she confronted a tower of abandoned wet laundry. Ever responsible, she stayed for three hours, drying and folding the sheets and towels. When we returned, Martha delivered an ultimatum. "I cannot work with her," she stated. No drama or outrage, simply a fact. If Cleo remained on the staff, Martha would be seeking other employment.

There was no mulling over this decision. It was clear which of my two housekeepers were expendable.

If I'd been unsettled by the prospect of hiring employees, you can imagine how I felt about having to *fire* one. Fortunately, Cleo made it easier for me. She disappeared for a week without notice. She finally called with a barrage of excuses; one being that she had been hospitalized with terminal cancer. By then I had learned from a mutual acquaintance that she'd run off to Chicago with a boyfriend. That sounded more plausible.

I never had to use the words, "you're fired." Instead, I explained in a sorrowful voice, "Cleo, I had to replace you."

"But Pat, you know I love my job," she protested lamely. But she understood, and was neither defensive nor defiant. We parted ways amicably, and I wished her well.

Martha recruited her friend Sonia, a big-hearted woman in her fifties who had two grown children. She came to the U.S. from Panama, and gets very excited when she encounters Hispanic guests with whom she can converse in Spanish. Martha, by the way, is fluent in Swahili. I'm the only one of us who's not bilingual.

Sonia came with ten years' housekeeping experience at a bed and breakfast across town. With a paring knife, she can slice an upright strawberry to look like an unfurling rosebud in a fruit centerpiece. She showed us how to fold the hand towels into hanging pockets in which she tucked the washcloths, fanned like seashells. Sonia also convinced Martha and me to fold the top square of the toilet paper into a triangle when preparing the guest bathrooms. I'd resisted this idea, thinking it made us look too hotel-like. Sonia set me straight. The toilet paper triangle signals to an incoming guest, "This room has been specially readied for you."

As our occupancy rates have grown, I've employed a number of other part-time housekeepers besides Martha and Sonia. Each of them has impressed me with their positive attitude and work ethic. Whenever one of them has left, it has always been to pursue a greater opportunity, like a full-time professional position or to enroll in college. I have maintained my perfect record of never firing anyone. And many of our former staff continue to keep in touch so I can follow their success.

Meanwhile, Martha and Sonia have remained constant for more than a decade. Martha enrolled in college, finished a degree, and is now a professional dental assistant while continuing to work part-time for us. I've watched her learn to drive, buy a car, buy a house, and become a U.S. citizen. Nearly two decades since emigrating from Kenya, Martha and Ali are typical American parents, monitoring their kids' homework and shuttling them to regional sports competitions. Shamim has emerged as a dynamo on the basketball court and at seventeen, is currently fielding scholarship offers from college coaches.

During the same period, Sonia's kids finished college with honors. Bob and I attended their graduation parties as well as Sonia's son Odell's wedding.

Soon after, we welcomed Joseph, her first grandson. Sonia's entrepreneurial daughter Leysi has launched a bilingual preschool center and I look forward to watching her business grow and prosper.

Our housekeeping staff has taught me a lot, and I'm not talking about stain removal. Each of us is born with a unique set of interests and talents. Chores I perceive as demeaning are a source of pride to other individuals. What I label boring, others find compelling.

My gratitude knows no bounds. It's said that people come into your life when you need them most (though I recognize, belatedly, I sure needed them in my twenties). They have raised the comfort level of the B&B beyond measure, not to mention my quality of life in general.

Notes to Aspiring Innkeepers

Thinking Beyond the Paycheck

Here's a puzzle: Why do people tip teenagers for the joy ride of valet parking, yet rarely leave a tip for housekeepers who labor for an hour in preparing their room? I can't bring myself to leave one of those conspicuously printed "thank you" envelopes, yet I wish guests were more thoughtful and proactive about tipping our housekeepers. It makes their day.

If you are like I was, confounded by the process of hiring employees and looking for ways to make them feel appreciated, here's what I've learned:

- Be selective. Choose staff based on their attitude and commitment. Skill can be accrued over time. Look for people who seem to share your values and work ethic.

- Employ two or more part-time staff rather than one full-time, so that you have extra resources if one calls in sick or schedules a vacation.

- Ask for their input on the cleaning supplies they prefer. Purchase tools and products to make their work easier.

- Emphasize excellence over speed. It's better to have a job done right than quickly.

- Create a checklist for every room and let staff check each other. Make the final inspection yourself. Even the most conscientious workers miss a detail or two.

- Make extra portions of their favorite breakfast entrée and send the leftovers home with them.

- Give them first dibs on the furniture, linens, or dishes you've decided to replace or donate.

- Always offer praise and appreciation along with criticism. Catch your employees doing things *right*.

- Remember their birthdays, and reward exceptional work with gifts and bonuses.

- Finally, introduce guests to the staff when the opportunity arises, in the same way that you would introduce guests to other guests. Let them know that the staff is not peripheral, but integral to your operation, and how much you value their service.

ELEVEN

Answering Service

I can't write about "Help!" without mentioning our assistant innkeepers. This succession of bright, personable University of Michigan students has contributed greatly to the seamless operation of the inn and to my peace of mind during the hours they are in charge.

In the beginning, I wanted nothing to do with them.

Natalie and Allyn were U-M seniors who had been working for Edith, the prior innkeeper, when we bought the place. They came in from 3:00 to 7:00 p.m. on alternate afternoons to take reservations and check in arriving guests. While Edith had been tepid about recommending Cleopatra, she thought highly of Natalie and Allyn. "Very reliable and responsible," she assured me, "and they would like to continue working for you."

I conceded that the housekeepers were indispensable—there was no way I could turn over nine bedrooms in a day by myself—but office help seemed like an extravagance. Surely I should be answering my own phone. Once again I was reverting to a lifelong habit, an inclination to *do* instead of to delegate.

Bob was more pragmatic. We needed coverage for large blocks of time so that we could be away from the inn, he argued, even if only to buy groceries. So I fell back on another lifelong habit, which was to give in to his better judgment.

Looking back, I should never have been skeptical. In 2003, Natalie and Allyn had more experience in running a B&B than I did.

In fact, the young people who've worked here over the past decade have had more experience than me in a number of areas, starting with technology. As millennials, they grew up with computers. "Do you know how to create a spreadsheet?" I once asked Jordan, a senior who was majoring in international marketing. She rolled her eyes and said kindly, "Pat, I learned to do that in preschool."

So when interviewing students for a staff opening, I skip over computer skills. That would be like asking, "Do you know how to walk?" Instead, I try to gauge their interest in working here, seeking a response like "I love meeting new people and making them feel welcome." Their resumes offer clues to their work ethic. I hired Gratiana partly because she was a member of the Michigan Marching Band. That spoke volumes about her initiative and commitment. Under the heading, "Demonstrated Abilities," Lauren wrote, "able to lift fifty pounds." This was incidental compared to her personality and people skills, but has certainly been useful when I return from Costco with eight crates of bottled water. The interview is more about getting to know a potential employee than grilling them about experience. When the conversation turns to cooking and I hear "chocolate chip cookies are my specialty," the meeting is over. They're hired.

The students anticipate this will be "a fun place to work," and proceed to make it so. They enliven it for me with their diverse perspectives. They think about things that are off my radar. To illustrate, here's a conversation with Natalie not long after we purchased the inn. She's a strikingly pretty young woman with glossy brown hair and luminous eyes.

"Um, Pat, there's something I've been wanting to talk to you about but I've been nervous about bringing it up. There is something I really, really want to do, and I've been thinking about it for a long time. But I don't want to lose my job if I do it."

Long suspenseful pause as she awaited my reaction. I couldn't imagine where this conversation was going.

"I want to do my hair in dreadlocks."

Dreadlocks?

I understood why she was seeking permission. Dreadlocks are more than fashion; they're a statement, and a controversial one at that. But she needn't have worried. College communities are a bastion of diversity and individual expression. "Go for it," I told her. Wasn't I already okay with the pierced eyebrow and the nose ring?

The dreadlocks ran their course. Within a few weeks, Natalie popped in with a pixie cut.

She and Allyn were very conscientious, but I couldn't help noticing that except for the occasional check-in or phone call, I was mostly paying them to study and cruise the Internet. But whose fault was that? They would have gladly taken on more tasks if I'd asked them, and were certainly capable. Both of them went on to earn law degrees and became practicing attorneys. They could not have been more accommodating, yet I could not bring myself to ask them to empty the dishwasher.

Fortunately, I had subsequent chances to rewrite the roles and raise expectations. Natalie and Allyn were merely the benchmark, my management training wheels. Unlike Martha and Sonia, loyal for more than a decade, students have an annoying tendency to graduate. And the turnover has played to my advantage. With each new hire, I've expanded the job description.

"Interacting with guests is your most important role," I explain to an applicant, "but I'm also counting on you for some pretty mundane tasks, like putting away groceries and refilling the hot tub."

Now our assistant innkeepers—we created a title that conveys status and looks good on their resumes—do just about everything, from managing reservations and orienting guests to the campus, to shoveling snow and schlepping groceries. They're ready to make up an extra twin bed when the couple we expected turns out to be a mother and son. They assemble furniture and yes, they empty the dishwasher. Nothing is too menial or too challenging.

Shrinking My Role

It's no mystery why people like me resist delegating. "It's easier to do it my-self" is our rationalization. If I do it, I'll know it's done right. But when Kim, our fourth student hire (who also went on to law school, by the way; is there a pattern here?) asked if she could help by assembling a quiche, I said sure. Turning over some of the food prep gained me hours of free time.

I let Kim choose the recipe and did not hover. My best-ever boss in Ki-nesiology, Dee Edington, never micromanaged. His philosophy was to hire good people and set them loose, which is how I left Kim in the kitchen. What a payoff! Her broccoli-and-cheddar quiche turned out way tastier than my version. The reason? Sautéed onions. Never again would my breakfast dishes exclude sautéed onions. Delegating is not only time-saving but highly instructive.

Kim bequeathed to us her cousin Marissa, who remained with us for a record four-and-a-half years. Timid when she began as a freshman, Marissa surprised us (and her parents) by announcing she had found a summer volun-teer job in Gambia. In successive summers she traveled to Hungary, Prague, Malaysia, and other countries. I got to vicariously experience her adventures, discovering also the myriad opportunities that have opened to idealistic young graduates. Two former staff, Natalie and Andrew, entered the Peace Corps, and a third, Bailey, is teaching in Thailand. Through Naomi, we learned about WWOOF, which stands for World Wide Opportunities on Organic Farms.

Laura Lapidus, a U-M theater major, alerted me to all of her performances where I sat front row center, as proud as a stage mother. Laura Langberg—actually there have been three Lauras and two Laurens in my employ, but I digress—made a tangible contribution to breakfast. What would I do without Laura's mother's Crustless Quiche, now one of our staples? Prior to this of-fering, making quiche was a two-step process involving lining the pan and prebaking the dough. *Crustless* quiche can be assembled in minutes from a dozen eggs, milk, and whatever cheese and chopped vegetables I happen to have on hand. A quarter-cup of flour gives it just enough heft to be cut into firm wedges, saving time, cost and calories. No one has ever complained to me about missing the crust.

After eliminating the crust, it was a short step to eliminating myself.

In 2012, Jordan, assistant innkeeper number eleven (or was she the eighth or fourteenth?) was approaching graduation without a job offer, like many of her classmates. This was concerning to her but an advantage to us, as we did not want to lose her. "What if we extended your hours and increased your pay," Bob proposed, "and you can continue working here through the summer while you continue your job search?" Her new responsibilities would include serving breakfast several mornings a week.

Wait a minute. Wasn't that *my* role? Whether at 7:00 a.m. for a single early riser or at 9:00 a.m. for a crowd on weekends, breakfast had been my exclusive domain. I'd honed the presentation, down to the angle of spoons in the jam jars, the ratio of English muffins to croissants in the breadbasket. I enjoyed orchestrating this daily feast and was wary about giving it up.

But with Jordan trained to oversee all of our operation *including* breakfast, Bob and I could get away for longer trips, knowing the inn would run smoothly in our absence.

So I agreed, and indeed, it felt weird to stay working at my computer on the first morning that Jordan took over, hearing her moving about the adjacent kitchen, frying up eggs, and chatting with guests.

My discomfort lasted five, maybe ten, minutes. It was astonishing how quickly I adjusted to liberation.

I've retained charge over Sunday, our most elaborate breakfast. But letting our assistants handle weekdays has been good for me and great for our guests. Whereas I fell into the habit of offering "eggs fixed whatever way you'd like," or (if I was feeling magnanimous) "a cheese omelet," my student chefs were more generous. Surveying the fridge contents, Naomi would say. "for an omelet, we have Swiss cheese, cheddar or feta. I can add onions, tomatoes, mushrooms, spinach, broccoli, green or red peppers, chopped ham or bacon…" the list would go on. If the mesmerized guest replied, "all of those sound great," she would not flinch. Naomi's omelets were packed like an exploding burrito. On the days she made pancakes, she offered a choice of eleven different toppings.

The assistant innkeepers are proactive. They stock the beverage refrigerator and snack basket, alerting me when we are running low on supplies. Gratiana sees blackened bananas as a cue to make banana bread. Andrew took the initiative to compose nine late-arrival letters, customized by room. Zealous to the point of obsessive, he also alphabetized the DVD collection and arranged the refrigerator magnets in a grid.

Our B&B guests tend to be young married couples, mid-level careerists, rising academics, and traveling retirees. Without our student employees, I might never encounter the eighteen to twenty-one-year-old demographic, or their unique interests and viewpoint. They've taught me to text (though I still prefer email) and expanded my music interests. Without them, I'd still be stuck in the sixties with Peter, Paul and Mary and the Beach Boys.

Guests who are here on university business appreciate the insider views of our staff. Parents bringing their high school-aged kids on a campus tour especially welcome the chance to interact with authentic students. And so do I.

Now, I cannot imagine running the B&B without the assistant innkeepers. Being an innkeeper, like few other occupations besides parenthood, is 24/7. The students enable us to get away from the place on a daily basis.

I call it burnout prevention.

> Jordan introduced me to "FOMO," meaning "Fear of Missing Out." It's the anxiety that something great is happening elsewhere and you're not part of it. Thanks to Jordan and her cohort, I'm not experiencing FOMO at all. They've made my life full.

Speaking of Guests

People. Ya gotta love 'em.

I mean you *really* have to *love* them.

Not just tolerate them or put up with them. If you choose to be an innkeeper, you had better take delight in all of your fellow humans be they charming or obnoxious. This can't be hired out or delegated. It's the single non-negotiable qualification for running a bed and breakfast.

We are the golden retrievers of the hospitality industry. We like practically everybody.

Of course, we prefer congenial to contentious. Who doesn't? But if you're grumpy, we won't take it personally. You're probably just having a bad day. If you're weird, we'll call you eccentric. And if you're downright annoying, and you happen to be staying at my B&B, I won't hold it against you. You'll make a great story for the next book.

Meet Henry, a case in point. He was a short, stocky dentist from Pittsburgh, visiting campus for his son's fraternity weekend. I noticed that Henry was extremely chatty, a true extrovert, when he checked in on the previous evening. This wasn't surprising. After all, dentists spend their days making one-way conversations with open-jawed patients who are unable to do more than grunt in response.

The following morning, I was feeling relaxed because no one had requested an early breakfast. With practice, I had streamlined the process so that it took exactly sixteen minutes to set out the plates and bowls, beverages, breads, fruit, cereal, and so forth. At 7:50 a.m. I was cutting it close, but what were the odds that any of our guests would appear precisely at eight? This was my way of living on the edge.

My reverie was broken by approaching footsteps.

Murphy's Law states, "if anything can go wrong, it will." For an innkeeper, this means if you are running behind schedule, you are certain to be interrupted.

Into the kitchen popped Henry, just as I was breaking eggs into pancake batter. He was wearing flip-flops and an orange T-shirt that said "Old Guys Rule." "How's it going?" he boomed, hoisting himself up on the Mexican-tiled counter top. *The man was actually sitting on my kitchen counter!* I opened the refrigerator and withdrew a carton of milk, trying not to lose momentum. But Henry was oblivious.

"Great place you have here," he persisted, his legs dangling. "So, whatever made you decide to start a bed and breakfast?"

My heart sunk as I had no choice but to respond. An innkeeper's day is often a sequence of interruptions, and this one was off and running.

I look back on Henry's invasion—I mean, appearance—with more humor than irritation. He was just being friendly. He assumed I craved company. When he asked, "how's it going?" he really wanted to know.

Curiosity is a hallmark of B&B guests, and I'm happy to satisfy it. If only I could implant an audiotape and push "play" in response to those same inevitable questions:

"Has this place always been a bed and breakfast?"

"What did you do before you became an innkeeper?"

"Isn't it a lot of work?"

"Are you ever able to get away?"

Any of these topics can elicit a very lengthy monologue. I've learned to respond with the condensed versions so as to quickly toss the conversational ball back into their court. I'm way more interested in hearing my guests' stories than retelling my own.

Abandon All Expectations

While the questions guests ask are predictable, almost everything else about guest behavior is *un*predictable. Each day unfolds like improv theater with an ever-changing cast of characters and no script. You don't even know when the show will begin.

If incoming guests said to expect them at three, they might show up at noon, or just as likely at seven. If they told us seven, it could be midnight. Of course, travel is always subject to weather delays and flight cancellations, and we could usually get updates by calling the guests' cell phones, which are duly noted in our reservation system. (We still record home phone numbers as a backup, but are finding that landlines are going the way of the telegraph and carrier pigeon.) Though we'd much rather greet late arrivals in person, no one has ever objected to receiving a note and a key under the front doormat. In fact, guests tell us that following a string of prominent signs with their names and arrows pointing to their rooms, like a trail of bread crumbs, feels personal and welcoming.

Similarly, the *time* that guests say that they would like to have breakfast has no relation to the time when they actually appear at the table.

"Breakfast is from 8:00 to 9:30," I tell arriving guests, "unless you need it earlier."

"Oh, that's fine," they assure me, citing travel fatigue and the intention to "sleep in." So who do you think I find milling around the kitchen at seven the next morning?

Or more often, it is the reverse. An ambitious guest requests breakfast at seven and I dutifully rise early to set out the full buffet an hour ahead of schedule. No one shows up. It seems Mr. Seven A.M. overslept and rushed off without eating, leaving me feeling like a teenager who's been stood up for a date. Or a hostess who's given a party to which nobody came.

Sometimes, those guests who insist on a 7:00 a.m. breakfast will dawdle in after eight, and it's so tempting to make a teasing wisecrack. But sarcasm is risky. You can never, ever let guests think they have inconvenienced you in the slightest. That's why when anyone asks, "Isn't this a lot of work?" I assure them it's not. Most of the time, I even believe it.

The best compliment we can receive, and the one we hear most often is "this feels just like home." (It's probably that pile of newspapers I haven't picked up from the sofa.)

The comparison is pleasing but it's just off the mark. What we *really* want our guests to be thinking is, "this feels just like *mom's* home."

Home is where you feel relaxed and secure. *Mom's home* is where you not only feel relaxed and secure, but cherished and cared for. Mom's home is where you awaken to the aroma of hot coffee, sizzling bacon, and bread just out of the oven. Coffee, bacon, and bread that you did not have to make for yourself. Mom's home is where someone other than you laundered the sheets, made the bed, and placed milk and cookies on the nightstand.

Here's how I can tell that guests think our B&B feels like home:

- After finishing breakfast, they clear their own plates and deposit them in the kitchen.
- Before I manage to stop them, some guests begin washing their own dishes.
- Every so often, someone shows up for breakfast in pajamas!

The More the Merrier

Naturally, we sought advice from other experienced innkeepers when we decided to open the Ann Arbor B&B in 2003. Alice, whose enthusiasm was waning after ten years in the business, issued a warning: "Never rent rooms to more than two people who know one another," she declared ominously. "They can take over your whole place."

I pretended to consider this notion. But when six lively women in their fifties, former college housemates, approached us about renting the B&B for a girlfriend getaway, I did not hesitate. Who would want to turn down a lucrative multiple-room booking? When they asked if they might hire a massage therapist and set up a spa in the living room, I said sure, since they were our only guests that weekend. I also agreed to a catered lunch and their seventies' CD soundtrack, dominated by Led Zeppelin and The Who. As Alice predicted, the women took over the place. But they were having a blast, and their joy was contagious. I might not abide this much revelry every weekend, but every once in a while, it can be highly entertaining.

Part of the allure of a bed and breakfast is that it brings people together. Because they are intimate and homelike, B&Bs are conducive to open communication and bonding. Ours has been the setting for advisory board meetings, staff retreats, and all kinds of family reunions. These groups have indeed been known to congregate in the living room and play board games all evening. Or share one or several six-packs on our balcony until two in the morning.

We're kind of delighted when that happens.

Some of my best memories are of times are when we were filled with guests gathered for a wedding, which often included the parents and grandparents, bridesmaids and groomsmen, and often the wedding couple themselves. I loved these occasions, with everyone in high spirits and the B&B ringing with stories and laughter. We'd be asked to take photos of the group in their finery. Then off they would go to the ceremony and the reception, leaving us in delicious solitude. The next morning at breakfast, we'd hear all the wonderful details.

While every wedding is special, the Bulgarian wedding stands out as one of the most memorable.

We'd been open only a few months when the bride booked all of our rooms for their big day. She was American, and she had met her Bulgarian fiancé while working abroad. His relatives spent a week with us prior to the wedding, and not a one of them spoke English. No matter, the young couple joined the groom's family for breakfast and served as interpreters. The rest of the time, we all communicated with sign language. The Bulgarians were exuberant but not rowdy, even entertaining us one evening with their musical instruments. And we picked up an important piece of Bulgarian culture, though we've yet to put it into practice. When drinking a shot of vodka, you must down it with a slice of cucumber.

Many Roads Lead to Ann Arbor

Because the university draws an international following, our visitors come from a world-wide radius. Our friends Melissa and Jim Tinney gave us a three-by-five-foot map of the seven continents, which I had dry mounted on foam core and hung near the entryway. It is now studded with multicolored pins indicating the cities our guests have come from—a bit sparse in Greenland and Russia, but dense throughout Europe, parts of Asia, and all of North America.

The most sophisticated guests take a childlike delight in choosing a color and positioning their pins. "Where I was born, or where I'm from now?" they ask. "Whichever place you think of as home," I respond. Often, they choose the place which is least represented, where their pin will stand out. An Irish guest who was living in Brooklyn elected to honor his birthplace in Ireland, but I'd run out of pins. "No problem," he said with a smirk. "I'll just steal one away from England."

Inevitably, someone asks wonderingly, "Do the pins represent all of the places you've been to?" Are they serious? We couldn't travel that much in ten lifetimes. And though we manage short getaways to see friends and relatives, for the time being, we are tethered to the B&B. And that's fine. The world comes to us.

The University also attracts world-class dignitaries and counts Mike Wallace, James Earl Jones, and Google founder Larry Page among its alumni. You might think we play host to the gifted and famous, such as the parade of performers appearing at the nearby Power Center and Hill Auditorium. This book could have been a celebrity tell-all! But in our experience, high-profile entertainers and artists really prefer the anonymity of a hotel suite over a sociable B&B. Performers spend so much time being on in front of an audience, that during their downtime, I suspect that they treasure their privacy.

A case in point: the U-M Business School brought a renowned economist to campus for a series of seminars. They booked him in our most requested room, Maine Woods, which has a kitchenette and skylights. Bob and I ordered the economist's latest book (in hardcover, no less) and speed-read it so that we could appear somewhat knowledgeable when we spoke with him. But that conversation never happened. The gentleman never appeared for breakfast or even for coffee. Following each lecture, he secluded himself in his room behind the "Do Not Disturb" sign. He clearly would have been happier at the Marriott.

Our VIP deficit is more of a relief than a disappointment. Famous people intimidate me. I was thrilled to watch comedian (and banjoist) Steve Martin perform at Power Center across the street with the Steep Canyon Rangers, but if Steve and his band had booked rooms at our B&B, I would have passed out when they checked in. This is not a worldly way to greet an icon.

But, was that the actor Rick Moranis browsing our DVD rack in the living room? Did he come here under an assumed name? The likeness was startling.

Our reservation system identified him as Sam Davis, a high school physics teacher from Cleveland. He was attending a conference on thermodynamics. I sidled up and couldn't help asking him, "So, how often do people tell you that you look like the actor in *Honey, I Shrunk the Kids?*"

He turned his familiar geek-like face toward me and sighed, "that's not exactly a compliment." Then he whipped out his cell phone and pressed the speed dial. "You've got to tell my girlfriend what you just said to me."

He handed over the phone and waited as I repeated the comment, hoping she wouldn't take offense. The voice at the other end laughed. "He's always telling me that. People are always mistaking him for Rick Moranis. I keep telling him, 'Honey, you look just like Tom Cruise to me.'"

Two of our best-known guests were not merely famous but infamous. A Chicago couple, Bill Ayers and Bernadine Dohrn, rented all of our B&B rooms for their son's wedding party. Ayers co-founded the radical Weatherman Underground when he was a Michigan student. The group was linked to bombing the Pentagon and the Capitol in the early 70s. His wife, also a member of the Underground, was at one time on the FBI's Ten Most Wanted list.

Decades later, they could not be more mainstream; Bill was an elementary education theorist and emeritus professor at University of Illinois at Chicago, and Bernadine was a law professor and director of the Children and Family Justice Center at Northwestern University. Watching Bernadine, wearing a flowing mother-of-the-groom dress, straightening Bill's tuxedo bow tie, you would never imagine them as a pair of 60s radicals. They were just your typical average happy parents celebrating their offspring's wedding.

Outside of the Ordinary

Have I overused the word "typical," as in "typical guests" or "typical morning?" That's a mistake. Each person is unique, and every occasion has the potential to take us by surprise.

For example, I've described people who choose B&Bs as generally outgoing and gregarious (like Henry the dentist). That's not to imply that the rest are unsociable introverts. But it's often the case that, especially on a leisurely Sunday, guests connect over shared interests, return several times to the buffet table, and talk long after the dishes have been cleared. It's a synergy I can count on. Unlike the host of a political fundraising event, I've never had to "work the room."

Yet like all sweeping generalizations, this one has been easily upended.

Often, the first or second guest who sits down to breakfast sets the tone. For example, one morning I greeted a husband and wife who had mentioned they had come for a medical appointment. They took their plates to the far end of the table and began talking to each other in hushed voices. When a third guest entered the room, the couple did not look up. Taking that as a cue, the guest poured a mug of coffee and reached for a section of the *New York Times*. Following suit, three more people sat down to breakfast and burrowed intently into their mobile phones.

Observing this from the kitchen, Bob said to me under his breath, "It's like a group of monks who have taken a vow of silence."

✻ ✻ ✻

Occasionally, someone will ask, "What was your *worst* guest experience?" I don't have to think twice about this one.

It happened over commencement weekend, the first year after we opened. The parents of one of the new graduates had asked if they could host a small reception, and we readily agreed. Their daughter, in cap and gown, and a dozen relatives and friends gathered the next evening to enjoy wine and cheese in our living room.

Suddenly, even over the din of conversation, we heard a commotion in the room directly above us. The occupants were an elderly couple who said they'd come to see their grandson graduate occupied it. Although they had seemed cheerful enough when they checked in earlier, they were now having an argument that was escalating into a screaming match.

I loathe conflict. My preferred way of dealing with conflict is to avoid it all costs, but this one was inescapable. As the reception group grew quiet and gazed upward with fascination, I felt a growing sense of panic. Finally, my husband called loudly, "May we help you?" The fracas subsided. "Sorry," came a voice from upstairs. "My wife got champagne in her eye. We'll be fine." Mercifully, the combatants remained quiet for the rest of the evening and slipped out the next morning before breakfast.

When our housekeeper went upstairs to turn over the room, she found that one of the pair had pulled the rollaway bed from the closet and slept on it.

It's A Small World After All

Finally, I'll relate one of our *best* guest experiences.

On a fall football weekend, two couples who had never met struck up a conversation across the breakfast table. They were parents of U-M undergraduates, eagerly comparing notes on their children's campus experience, but two of them were about to discover that they had much more in common. "You have an unusual accent. Where are you from?" Lewis asked the woman across from him. "Pauls Valley, Oklahoma," Jeannie drawled, with a broad smile. "It's a tiny little town. You'd never have heard of it."

Lewis stared at her. "*I'm* from Pauls Valley myself," he declared.

Over the next hour they (and we) learned that Jeannie and Lewis had gone to the same high school two years apart, and knew many of the same people. They had been to the same shops and eateries. Learning Jeannie's last name, Lewis exclaimed, "I dated your sister!"

Sure, people meet over breakfast and discover they're both from Chicago. But Pauls Valley, Oklahoma, population 6,000? What are the odds of this happening?

One of the group had brought a camera, and Bob took photos of the four of them, but he warned, "When you get the film developed, you'll find that it's blank. You were never at this B&B and this meeting never happened. It's all an episode from the *Twilight Zone.*"

What's more, there's a postscript. Three years later, we were telling this story at a dinner party in Laguna Beach, California. One of the guests looked at us wryly and said, "My mother grew up in Pauls Valley, Oklahoma."

Connections and coincidences are frequent here, if rarely this dramatic. A B&B is a crossroads where many guests discover an amazing number of common interests and shared experiences. It's thrilling, actually, to hear gales of laughter coming from what had been a table of eight strangers. As innkeepers, we're focused on relations with our guests. But it's just as exciting to see guests relate to each other.

You know that your guests have transitioned to friends when:

* They call you en route and say, "We're stopping at Whole Foods on our way in. Would you like us to pick up anything?"

* You receive a Christmas card with photos and their family news update.

* They friend you on Facebook.

* They invite you to stay in *their* home. If you're ever in Ottumwa, Iowa, the guestroom is ready and waiting. And they can hardly wait to make you breakfast.

Notes to Aspiring Innkeepers

Everyone We Meet Becomes a Part of Who We Are

None of your friends are likely to say to you, "I sure wish my home had twelve bathrooms." Or envy your five-figure annual grocery bill.

But you'll hear this again and again: "You must meet the most interesting people."

And they're right. You can only smile in agreement.

Rarely will you find a profession that brings you in touch with such a wide range of people on an almost daily basis as innkeeping. They not only enrich your life with their stories and experience, but thank you profusely for adding to theirs. And then they hug you warmly when they leave. Really, can you think of a profession in which you may be hugged, up to a dozen times, on a daily basis?

THIRTEEN

And Now...Drum Roll... The BreakFEST

Eat breakfast like a king, lunch like a prince, dinner like a pauper.
-- Adelle Davis, American nutritionist and writer

How many times have we heard and repeated this advice? It's the rule here in the B&B kingdom, where breakfast reigns. It is our niche of the hospitality industry. Breakfast is what sets us apart from motels, hotels, and RV campgrounds.

Think about it: without breakfast, we would be merely a "bed." Compare:

1. *Ann Arbor Bed and Breakfast*
2. *Ann Arbor Bed*

Number 2 sounds like a mattress store.

Chain lodging sites have certainly noticed the allure of breakfast as an extra added attraction and many now promote it among their amenities. They've even commandeered the words "bed and breakfast" in their promos. But honestly, have you checked out what they are offering? Here's what I've found: cellophane-wrapped pastries and bagels, tubes of cream cheese, bottled juices, and boxes of cold cereal. Occasionally there might be a chafing dish of rubbery scrambled eggs and sausage, and that's usually (if at all), on weekends only.

No contest. B&Bs do it so much better! Our breakfasts are fresh, imaginative, and memorable. Since becoming an innkeeper, I stayed in B&Bs whenever I traveled (a business expense known as research) and encountered such delights as:

- poached eggs over smoked salmon in a puff pastry nest
- parfait glasses layered with fresh berries and crème fraiche
- crunchy melt-in-your-mouth pecan waffles with 100 percent real Michigan maple syrup

I am getting hungry just writing about this.

Truth in Advertising

Before we became innkeepers, making breakfast seemed to me an arcane activity of my distant past, like blind dates and downhill skiing. I phased it out as soon as my daughter and son became old enough (aged six and three) to open a box of Fruit Loops and pour their own milk. I didn't feel negligent. I was a conscientious mother producing self-reliant children.

As for me, I skipped breakfast altogether, erroneously believing that saving calories in the morning was a shrewd weight loss strategy. (It didn't work. It made me ravenous for lunch and dinner.)

Yet when I stopped to think about it, breakfast was my favorite meal. I could eat Eggs Benedict three times a day, and hopefully survive the triple bypass. So menu planning for our B&B venture was—and still is—one of my greatest pleasures.

I aimed to be honest in describing it, however. So many B&Bs seem to tout their "gourmet breakfast." Doesn't this raise unrealistic expectations? (To be honest, I've never served *anything* in a puff pastry nest.) The Food Network was not pressing me to compete on Iron Chef. I wasn't comfortable with a G for Gourmet rating, and skipped to H, the next letter of the alphabet. Healthy and Hearty are the words that more accurately describe our breakfast.

✻ ✻ ✻

"What *time* is breakfast?" guests asked on arrival, a fair question. Destination B&Bs can dictate when breakfast is served, declaring a very specific "seating" time. I once stayed at a country inn where guests were told to gather in the drawing room prior to 9:00 a.m. There we waited in suspense until precisely 9:00, when the doors leading into to the dining room parted and we were ushered to our tables. It was an elegantly orchestrated experience, but not one I'm inclined to emulate. Our guests, especially those during the weekdays, have agendas. We need to be flexible, so here's how it goes:

Guest 1 checks in.
> **Us:** Breakfast tomorrow is from 8:00 to 9:30. Will that work for you?
> **Guest 1:** Actually, I have to be at a meeting by 8:30.
> **Us:** No problem, we can easily have breakfast out at 7:30.

Guest 2 checks in.
> **Us:** ...and breakfast tomorrow is from 7:30 to 9:30. Will that work for you?
> **Guest 2** (looks at his itinerary): Gee, it looks like I'm being picked up at 7:30.
> **Us:** We'll set up breakfast at 7:00. See you at 7:00.

Guest 3 checks in.
> **Us:** Breakfast tomorrow is from 7:00 to 9:00. Will that work for you?

Of course, sometimes the timing moves in the opposite direction. For travelers coming to Ann Arbor from the west coast, 7:00 a.m. means 4:00 a.m. No problem. If someone happens to sleep through breakfast and appear after the food has been cleared, I am happy to pull it out again.

It's easier to be flexible in your practices and policies than to obsess over setting up rules and defending them. The more flexible you are, the more likely your guests will feel relaxed and at home.

Musical Chairs

A second decision involved seating arrangements. I originally planned to fill the dining area with small round bistro tables for two, like a little café. Then at an antiques market, Bob and I spotted a gleaming six-foot long Heywood Wakefield table with two extensions and eight matching chairs. It fit perfectly with the mid-century modern theme of our home. More than that, I realized, it suited the ambiance we were seeking to create. Guests would have isolated themselves at the individual tables, but were drawn together at the table for eight. We added a smaller table for the overflow and crossed our fingers that guests would come to breakfast sequentially rather than arrive all at once. This usually proved to be the case.

The table for eight really does promote camaraderie, just as we'd hoped. Most mornings, even the most introverted visitors sit down, introduce themselves, and strike up a conversation with their fellow guests. Conversations among mathematicians are especially entertaining. They seem to speak in their own cryptic code.

Fellowship, as much as food, is central to the B&B experience.

Plates, Platters and Picnics

For a new innkeeper, the overriding question about breakfast was not just what to serve, but how to serve it. Hot or continental? Plated or buffet? This was the first I knew that "plate" is a verb well as a noun.

Notes to Aspiring Innkeepers

Solving the Dining Dilemma

Do you furnish the breakfast room with one long large table seating many, or several smaller tables for two or four? Large tables invite the spirited fellowship that many people associate with the B&B experience. But some innkeepers wonder if they might intimidate individuals or couples who prefer quiet privacy.

Solution: Hedge your bets and include both a large table for eight with one or two smaller tables, if space allows. Or consider three or four square tables that can be joined to form a larger one.

Plating a breakfast is much more economical. You, the cook, control the portions. I've stayed at B&Bs where the fruit consisted of a cantaloupe wedge. Two miniature muffins with honey made up the bread course, and no one complained.

A second advantage to plating is aesthetic. The plate is your canvas. A stack of pancakes looks brown and boring, but with a swizzle of syrup, a sprinkle of powdered sugar and a crown of berries, you can create a masterpiece. Garnishing and serving individual entrées takes a little more time, but enhances the guests' feelings of being pampered. "Plating" gives the innkeeper control over portion size, making the choice both elegant and cost-conscious.

But I am neither elegant nor, sorry to say, very cost-conscious, so we've opted to present breakfast as a buffet. The generosity of it suits our informal style. Besides, we really *do* serve twenty for breakfast most weekends, when all nine rooms are filled and some are outfitted with extra beds to accommodate three or four people. In addition, when parents are visiting students, we always invite the students for breakfast. The students sometimes invite a friend. More often, the students always happily accept and then fail to appear. It's the weekend, after all, and nine times out of ten, they opt to sleep in. The parents aren't surprised and neither are we. The invitation makes us look magnanimous and costs us nothing.

The point is, weekend breakfasts at the Ann Arbor B&B aren't just big; they're colossal. A typical entrée uses more than a dozen eggs; the baked French toast recipe calls for a full loaf of bread, not a few slices. We try to provide variety as well as quantity, figuring that the more choices we offer, the better to satisfy everyone's tastes.

A big bowl of chopped fruit is our centerpiece. Early on, we realized practically no one takes the time at home to mix together cantaloupe, strawberries, pineapple, blueberries, raspberries, nectarines, plums, pears, mango, star fruit, grapes, and kiwi for an everyday breakfast at home. I love the look of it, the wild conglomeration of color. And fruit is foolproof. The bacon can burn; the frittata can fail to set, but fruit, as long as it's fresh, turns out perfect every time.

Serving buffet style takes monitoring to make sure nothing runs short, but that sure beats shuttling individual plates back and forth from the kitchen. As a practical matter, I am happy to have the hungry crowd helping themselves to whatever appeals to them instead of waiting to be served what I designated. It does mean that guests will eat more and linger longer. You can almost hear the buffet table calling out in a seductive whisper: *"Want some more? Sure you do! Have a second (or third or fourth) helping!"*

Here's what we typically set out every day on our sprawling sideboard:

Beverages

Coffee (regular and decaf) in large thermal Air Pot dispensers; a pitcher of half-and-half

Tea (regular, herbal, de-caf varieties); hot water dispenser; honey, lemon

Sugar and artificial sweeteners

Hot chocolate mix

Fresh-squeezed orange juice

Some other kind of juice—usually cranberry-apple, or pink grapefruit

Pitcher of ice water

Breads and toppings

Bread basket—any combination of bakery breads, muffins, croissants, scones, etc.

Cake plate with coffee cake, banana bread or pastries

Jam in three flavors and colors, like blueberry, cherry and apricot

Butter

Cream cheese if there are bagels in the bread basket

Cereals, fruits, and milk

Cereal canisters—one with Kashi Strawberry Fields flakes; one with Cheerios, of course

Granola, home made from a local bakery

Chopped walnuts

Mixture of raisins and dried cherries

Fresh fruit salad

Plain low-fat yogurt

Assorted individual flavored yogurts

Skim milk

We have fewer guests on weekdays—there's typically just one person occupying each room, even when all of the rooms are filled. They tend to be business professionals, research collaborators, conference attendees. They've often indulged in a big dinner with colleagues the night before, and decide that the fare listed above is more than enough. When I offer to warm up a slice of quiche or whip up an omelet, a surprising number decline. Or

Notes to Aspiring Innkeepers

No Meat? No Dairy? No Gluten? No Problem!

"Don't be a short order cook," a long-time innkeeper advised me when we opened the business. She offered exactly one entrée, calling it "Cook's choice." The choice that she offered her guests might be summed up as "take it or leave it."

I get her point. Ask your guests "what would you like for breakfast?" and who knows where it can lead. A request for lobster bisque? Beef Wellington? Instead, offer options you're prepared to fulfill: "Would you prefer eggs or pancakes?" And brace yourself for the guest who asks for an omelet.

Be prepared for the guests who have allergies or dietary restrictions or preferences, by stocking the refrigerators and pantries with the following:

- Eggbeaters™ or egg whites

- Soy milk and/or almond milk in various flavors for those who are lactose intolerant

- Gluten free bread, granola, and other cereals. Gluten-free muffins if you want to go the extra mile.

These days, many people have food issues…or perhaps they are just more willing to mention them. Along with "why are you coming?" and "what time should we expect you?" it's imperative to ask potential guests about allergies and food preferences. It's to our advantage to be prepared, and people who have these sensitivities always appreciate being asked.

they hesitantly ask (as if concerned that they are putting me to a great deal of trouble) for scrambled eggs.

Here's a confession. I love making scrambled eggs. I love whisking them in the bowl as they turn a deep lemon yellow, adding a dash of seasoning and—here's the secret to making them fluffy—a splash of water, and then watching them turn from liquid to solid in the sputtering hot pan. What a great word, "scramble!" I would *pay* people to let me scramble an egg for them.

On weekends, when we typically have more guests with larger appetites, it makes sense to include a casserole entrée that can be prepared in advance. Recipes like Laura's Mother's Crustless Quiche and Baked Apple French Toast, which are found at the end of this book, can be made the day before and baked or heated in the morning. Scrambled eggs, or any other kind of eggs for that matter, are always available on request.

And what about those folks making pre-dawn departures? No eggs for them, unless they're hard boiled. But we do pack to-go bags for them, which might include:

* Fresh fruit
* Carton of yogurt
* Bottled juice, water or both
* Package of nuts, raisins or trail mix
* Granola bar
* Wrapped muffin or coffee cake
* Napkin, plastic cutlery
* Just to be decadent, two pieces of dark chocolate

One night I baked a loaf of banana pecan bread and left it to cool on the counter for a guest who said he'd be leaving at 5:00 a.m. Beside it was a plate, knife and napkins. The coffee maker was pre-set for his coffee to-go, and the note next to cellophane-wrapped banana bread said "Help yourself."

He did. He took the entire loaf.

Notes to Aspiring Innkeepers

Seven Steps to an Easy-Breezy Morning

If you were seeking a totally carefree lifestyle, you would not have decided to run a B&B. Still, you'll go a long way toward achieving it by prepping as much of the breakfast as possible the night before. For example, you can:

- Set the table

- Measure the coffee, ready to brew

- Slice the breads; wrap in plastic

- Slice butter for the butter dish

- Pre-cut melon, hull and slice strawberries, section citrus fruits and pineapple. Don't mix the fruit until morning. Strawberries, for example, "bleed" on pineapple chunks, and bananas turn brown unless added just before serving.

- Pre-assemble your main dish so it's ready to pop in the oven

- Set out bowls, juice glasses, mugs, plates, and a warming dish if you're planning to use one.

Preparing ahead shaves off minutes you'll be glad you have in the morning, when a guest shows up earlier than you expected.

Streamlines and Shortcuts

The steps above reduce stress in the morning, but they're more about time *shifting* than time saving. You're now devoting a chunk of the evening to table setting and slicing butter. We innkeepers have to find ways to increase our efficiency at all times. Why? Less time in the kitchen means more time for guests, and not incidentally, more time for ourselves.

So here's my mantra: think in terms of results, not processes. I'm a decent cook but a disaster at baking. My loaves of bread turn out heavy as lead (rhyme intended). I finally understand why: you can improvise on a baked egg entrée, adding extra seasonings, doubling the grated cheese, substituting broccoli for spinach. But you can't mess with bread dough. Change the ratio of yeast to flour and you alter the chemical interaction. Baking is all about chemistry, a course I skipped in high school because the teacher, the terrifying Mrs. Davenport, had a reputation for failing seniors, causing them not to graduate. I wasn't about to run that risk. I took typing instead.

> At my age, I'm not going to master the chemistry of bread-baking (or any number of other skills, like figure skating or conversational French). Ann Arbor has more than a dozen outstanding bakeries, and I've replaced baking with buying. I take a cue from my friend Mary Joscelyn, who once brought a fabulous layered pate to a dinner event. "Mary! Give us your recipe," we begged. To which Mary replied with a smile, "my talent is not in the preparation...but the procurement."

For those of us who still enjoy the preparation but want to minimize the minutes, here are some tips:

- Visit the salad bar section of your local supermarket and fill a container with the cooked bacon bits. You can add them to omelets or other egg dishes, saving the step of frying up raw strips of bacon for this purpose. Ounce for ounce, it's even less expensive.

- Chop onions and peppers, freeze on a cookie sheet so they don't stick together, then store in zip-lock bags in the freezer for a quick and colorful addition.

- Likewise, buy quantities of blueberries and raspberries in season, freeze on a cookie sheet, store in zip-lock bags to be added to pancakes or muffins.

- Got a favorite knife or whisk or spatula? Buy duplicates so that you always have one clean and ready.

- Wrap sets of silverware in napkins secured with a napkin ring so that you can provide place settings in a hurry when needed.

- Combine your favorite spices into your own signature seasoning mix, or try the recipe that follows.

Fine Herbs, Fine Friends, Life's Seasonings

My daughter Shannon and her husband Kevin were married at a potluck wedding. As favors, they gave shakers of this seasoning mix labeled with the sentiment above. The two of them experimented for weeks before settling on the following ingredients:

- salt
- basil
- parsley
- garlic powder
- onion powder
- Italian seasoning

Mix in equal proportions, store in an airtight container. Mix with olive oil for a dipping sauce, or use liberally on pasta, vegetables, and other entrees.

This flavorful seasoning mix is a great timesaver and a tasty addition to scrambled eggs, omelets and other savory breakfast treats.

FOURTEEN

Conquering Fear of Omelets

We'd been open less than a month when a guest turned to me at breakfast and asked in a hopeful voice, "Could you make me an omelet?"

He spoke with a slight accent, drawing out *ahmmmyoulette*, making the very word sound succulent and sacred.

I stared at him as if he had asked for pheasant under glass.

I had never made an omelet. How had I reached my sixties without mastering something so basic? I knew what they looked like. Our son Marc had taught himself how to make omelets when he was fifteen, and enjoyed treating us to his specialty on Sunday mornings. He made them so well; there was no reason for anyone else in the family to learn.

"Certainly," I told the guest, and managed to deliver a disheveled stir-fry of scrambled eggs, chopped spinach, and melted cheese. Then I set out to learn how to do it right.

As it turned out, omelets are so easy.

They do take practice and require the right tools, specifically a high quality non-stick frying pan. My top choice is a heavy-gauge, eight-inch Williams Sonoma pan with gently sloping sides. A nine- or ten-inch pan works, but produces a thinner and larger omelet. I also recommend a flexible rubber spatula.

Prepare ahead the ingredients you plan to offer as a filling so that they are ready to add, at room temperature. Two large eggs are standard and work well in an eight-inch skillet. Use a larger fry pan for a three or four egg omelet.

Various fillings may include:

- ⅓ cup grated cheese per two-egg omelet—American, Monterey Jack, Swiss, feta, or whatever. The majority of our guests choose sharp cheddar.
- Sautéed vegetables such as onions, mushrooms, broccoli, or asparagus
- Chopped fresh vegetables such as tomatoes, peppers, or spinach
- Herbs such as garlic, parsley, or dill
- Crisp bacon, chopped ham, or sausage

Whisk the eggs in a bowl, adding a dash of salt if desired. A splash of water—about a tablespoon per egg—will make the eggs fluffier.

Heat the pan after coating it with a teaspoon of melted butter or oil. When you see the butter or oil sizzling, pour in the beaten eggs. As the egg mixture quickly begin to set, lower the heat and push it gently toward the center of the pan with the spatula while allowing the uncooked mixture to fill the sides of the pan. Or, pull it away from the center and tilt the pan to fill in the gap.

When the eggs are nearly set, liberally sprinkle on the cheese so that it can begin to melt, followed by the desired fillings. Figure on about one-third to one-half cup of fillings (in addition to the cheese) for a two-egg omelet. Gently fold it in half or thirds, garnish with a pinch of fresh herbs, and serve. The omelet's heat will finish cooking the eggs and melting the cheese during the minute it takes to deliver the plate to the table.

Omelets are now my go-to entrée on mornings when there are too few guests to justify making a quiche or casserole. They are a great way to use the odd stalk of asparagus or half of a bell pepper in the fridge. Go elegant with smoked salmon or shrimp, or Southwestern with avocado and green chilies. The flavor possibilities are infinite.

FIFTEEN

Exceptions Rule

Like any good business, we deliberated carefully on rate structures, rules, and regulations at the time we opened. Were our policies set in stone? More like set in a bucket of water. The policy that has governed us most consistently is: this policy is subject to change.

My attitude toward some of the most basic aspects of our business keep shifting, and in many cases it's made a complete reversal. Here are a few of the matters I felt strongly about in the beginning:

- Our room rates are never discounted
- Cancellations require two-days' notice
- I will never display a "Vacancy" sign
- Children over ten are welcome
- Sorry, no pets

Discounts Available Upon Request

Our three-tier room pricing structure is pretty straightforward: the lower-priced rooms are smaller with queen beds. The next level of rooms has king beds and private balconies, and the premium rooms have extra amenities like kitchenettes, spa tubs, and skylights. The rooms are pictured and described in detail on our website, along with the nightly rate.

But not everyone checks the website. On a regular basis, we still get calls that begin, "How much are your rooms?" Or every innkeeper's favorite, "What's your cheapest room?" (I'm tempted to say $400, so the cost-oriented caller will simply gasp and hang up the phone.)

Sometimes I offer a room rate and the caller asks, "Can you do any better?" This seems rude and annoying. Our rates are not negotiable, I think indignantly. Would they go to a department store and say, "What's the lowest price you'd take for this sweater?"

But fellow innkeepers Jon and Linda Darrow, who once owned Saravilla B&B in Alma, MI, changed my mind. "If someone asks for a discount, I'm happy to knock off 10 percent," Jon says with a shrug. "It makes people feel good to think they're getting a bargain."

I've adopted his attitude. Mention AAA, AARP, your San Diego Zoo membership? We'll give you a discount.

Not only that, but if you call us at the last minute and the only room we have available that night is Ocean View with the king bed, kitchenette, and private patio with hot tub, you're in luck, because I won't be quoting you the rack price of $239. I'll likely offer the room for much less, because what's the point of letting it go empty? Similarly, if you've booked our lower priced Rainforest room but you arrive on a day when six other rooms are empty, we'll probably upgrade you to a larger room for the same price. Why not? It takes just as long to turn over a large room as it does a small one. To me, innkeeping is about maximizing service and value, not raising the bottom line.

Pardon the Short Notice

Every lodging establishment has a cancellation policy. Ours is pretty liberal; we merely ask that guests let us know within forty-eight hours of their arrival date if they are not coming. Football weekends and graduation have a longer lead-time—two months instead of two days—but guests who cancel within a shorter time frame are rarely penalized. Rooms are in high demand for event weekends. As soon as they're rebooked, the original guest's money is refunded.

When someone cancels a reservation for next month or next year, it feels inconsequential. When it's for next week, it feels like a blow. One canceled room means that about $200 in expected revenue is gone in a heartbeat. If losing one night's revenue is disappointing, losing a multiple night booking is calamitous. At the least, it's *very* inconvenient.

Our young guest Samantha had arrived early Sunday to take part in a University of Michigan program for high school graduates interested in medicine. She would be shadowing nurses and interns at U-M Hospital and exposed to a wide range of procedures and disciplines. We gave her a reduced room rate of $120 per night because she was staying for ten days and charged her newly-acquired credit card.

Bubbling with anticipation, Samantha settled into her room, showered, and then left for the afternoon's orientation. That evening she bounced into the kitchen where I was prepping the next morning's breakfast. She was wearing a crisp new Michigan T-shirt and a happy smile.

"I have the best news!" she announced. "One of the nurses I met has invited me to stay with her in her apartment this week. So I won't be needing the room after all!"

What she meant was, "I want you to rejoice in my good fortune and refund me $1,200."

I was not nearly as happy about this turn of events as Samantha.

Still, I enthused about how living with a medical professional would enhance her learning experience and then gently brought up our two-days' notice policy. I would refund most of her money, but not all of it.

"But I haven't really used the room," she whined. "Yes, but it was not available to anyone else because we were holding it for you," I explained patiently. This was a teachable moment.

Based on our two-day cancellation policy, I could have withheld the payments for Monday and Tuesday nights, but in the end, I only charged her for

Sunday. Three nights' rent seemed too stiff a penalty, and perhaps we would be able to rebook the room anyway.

I confess that I have a hard time charging for last minute cancellations. In most cases the reason is illness, although ironically, it's rarely the caller who's not feeling well. "My wife woke up with a 102 fever," the caller will say. Or, "My partner fell and twisted his ankle. I'm calling you from the emergency room." I've concluded that the ill and injured are simply too weak to make the call themselves.

The second most common reason for an eleventh-hour cancellation is death, and it's usually a grandmother. It's surprising how many elderly women drop dead just as their loved ones are about to leave for a weekend at our bed and breakfast.

Here's the dilemma: I'm at the other end of the phone, not standing beside the person who is dead or dying. I'm in no position to judge whether the caller is telling the truth or not, but I just can't respond with, "Tough luck. I'm charging your card."

"Vacancy" is Another Word for "Welcome"

At first, I resisted the notion of displaying a "Vacancy" sign at the B&B, concerned that it sent a negative message. If "No Vacancy" suggested that our rooms were in a high demand, then maybe "Vacancy" implied we were not popular.

Bob never followed this reasoning and took a pragmatic approach. We had an empty room. Why keep it a secret? Let's spread the word to all passing potential guests. He bought a 2 × 3 foot Vacancy sign off the rack at Ace Hardware, and skewered it into the ground next to the driveway. It promptly reeled in a Canadian couple driving from Toronto to Chicago. "We were headed for one of the hotels outside town but we saw your sign and thought a B&B might be more interesting," the wife said. Just like that, we gained two grateful overnight guests and money in our pocket. I never hesitated to hang that sign out again.

Tyke Patrol

There are two reasons we discourage parents from bringing babies and toddlers. First, the staircase and other structural features of the house pose a safety hazard for small people. Second, other guests, especially couples enjoying a romantic getaway from their *own* brood, are not expecting to encounter someone else's.

Still, "Children over ten welcome" is probably the rule we break most often, especially during low occupancy periods.

If someone is traveling with an infant, for example, we can offer one of the ground floor rooms that are relatively isolated and soundproof. We even have a Pack 'n Play.

When a caller mentions, "We have a daughter who's eight and a son who just turned five," I often respond, "No problem. Those two ages add up to more than ten. What do your kids like for breakfast?"

And how could we turn away the single mom who booked online, leaving the impression she was traveling alone, and then appeared in our doorway with an angelic four-year-old. The child peered up at me soulfully, clutching a stuffed rabbit. "Her father has custody, and I only get to fly in and see my daughter on weekends," the mother explained quietly. "I wanted us to spend our time together in a place that seemed more like a home than a hotel room."

Rules are made to be broken.

We also readily make exceptions when families book the entire B&B for gatherings such as weddings and reunions. If an infant or a toddler gets cranky, he'll be surrounded by solicitous aunts, uncles, and grandparents, ready to placate and comfort him.

Ultimately, our policy regarding children is not challenged too often, because most families traveling with kids tend to seek out one of the large chain hotels with an indoor pool. That's what I'd choose if I were in their place. Our living room is comfy but it's no match for a pool and a playground.

And then there are folks like Michael and Jennifer, who stayed with us on their wedding night and returned on their first anniversary and the two that followed. They moved out of state when Mike began graduate school, but always booked their favorite room with us on return visits to Ann Arbor. Then came the exciting news that they had adopted a baby. "We can't wait for you to meet Sidney," said Jennifer, who had already showered us with photos. I couldn't wait either. I certainly couldn't wait ten years.

So yes, we discourage guests from bringing small children, but stop way short of prohibiting them.

But We're Not a Kennel

Travelers sometimes call and ask if our B&B is pet friendly. Having been owned by a series of lovable dogs and cats over the years, I have great affection for animals. Our Old English Sheepdog, Mardi—short for Mardi Gras, as she was born in New Orleans—was elderly when we opened the B&B and she was an integral part of our operation.

Having a pet on the premises had plenty of pluses. True, we might have deterred some guests who had an aversion to animals, but just as many were likely to choose us because of Mardi's presence. They would walk into the door, absently hand over their credit cards, and look right past us calling, "Where's the dog? Where's the dog?" Mardi would rise to her feet (that is, paws), slowly walk toward the guests and lower her head to be petted. Then she'd return to the living room and resume her nap.

So when Mardi passed away, we missed her, and decided to designate one of our rooms for guests bringing pets. We chose Jamboree, a ground floor room which had a tile floor (no risk of accidents on the carpet) and an outdoor patio. What could go wrong?

We soon found out. The first couple to book pet-friendly Jamboree brought a high-strung Dalmatian. He became hysterical when they left him alone for an afternoon. He pawed and clawed the sliding screen door to the patio, leaving it a mangled wreck. This incident ended our short-lived experiment. We still accept humans but refer their pets to a congenial nearby kennel.

There are always exceptions. We welcome service dogs, like the docile German Shepherd who came with her owner for police officer training. Though barely a puppy, she didn't bark once and was better behaved than many guests I've encountered.

The other exception is Clara, a super-sociable, eighty-four-pound lab mix who accompanies our interim innkeeper Marcia Rockwood whenever she moves in to run the B&B in our absence. Clara almost invariably gets top mention in the guest diaries we leave in the rooms: "Thank you, Clara and Marcia for my wonderful stay…" the typical entry begins. The writer may mention the delicious food or the warm ambiance but invariably heaps the highest praise on Clara.

SIXTEEN

Online Review Sites:
The Power and The Perils

We are so lucky to be running a B&B in the age of the Internet.

Imagine being an innkeeper in the olden days—the early 1980s. Think of the marketing challenge: mailing press releases to travel editors, paying for advertisements in the Yellow Pages and various guidebooks; spending thousands of dollars printing tri-fold brochures and trucking them to welcome centers across the interstate. And there they'd sit in the display cases, competing for attention with flyers promoting wineries, museums, and the World's Largest Crucifix in Indian River, Michigan.

Instead, people simply find us via Google. If you type in the city "Ann Arbor" and "Bed and Breakfast," up pops our website, complete with a link to reviews. Now, motorists are even finding us on their smartphones as they approach the city. They can view the rooms, check for availability, and call us en route. If we have a vacancy, they can plug us into their GPS and sail right into our driveway. Technology makes it all so easy.

Once they find us on the Internet, it's often the reviews on TripAdvisor that seal the deal. Other review sites such as Google Places and Yelp are also influential, but TripAdvisor gets the most traffic. A high number of five-star reviews can put your B&B at the top of the lodging list. Guests read what other people say about their experiences and decide whether to book on that basis. TripAdvisor is an unbeatable marketing tool, and it costs us nothing.

Founded in 2000, the review site grew steadily in membership and influence over its first decade. By 2017, TripAdvisor Media Group operated twenty-five travel brands with names like Airfarewatchdog, BookingBuddy, CruiseCritic, and SeatGuru. It extends worldwide, claiming over one hundred million opinions and ratings of hotels, restaurants, and other travel-related attractions.

I was barely aware of TripAdvisor when we opened in 2003, and would not have dreamed of asking a guest to post a review. That would seem pushy. Gradually however, I noticed that other innkeepers were not so bashful, including several in my own community. Some smaller and newer B&Bs were boasting forty or fifty reviews, while we had garnered only a handful. Clearly it was time to be more assertive. Now, if a departing guest hands me the keys and says, "We love this place and we'll be back," I look them straight in the eye and ask, "Can you put that in writing?"

Third-party reviews sound much more credible than anything we could say about ourselves. They use words I could never apply without sounding conceited, like the reviewer who wrote, "The innkeepers are so nice and the place is adorable."

The headings alone can be a boon to your business even if no one reads the text:

"Great Location and Value"

"Quirky and Cute"

"Wonderfully Warm and Welcoming"

"Hospitality As If People Mattered"

"Comfortable, Colorful, Clean, and Convenient"

But I do read every word of the text and always find reviews constructive, whether they are reinforcing what we're doing right or indicating areas for improvement. For example, I questioned whether it mattered that we put out platters of home-baked cookies. Then I noticed that those cookies, along with other free snacks and beverages, were cited among the "extras" guests say they appreciate. We're still baking. The cookies are a keeper.

I like seeing our staff described as friendly and accommodating, and seeing the words "funky" and "fun" used to define our décor. "Home away from home" is a phrase that appears over and over.

Bob created a website, thankyouguest.com, that directly links to several review sites. It's printed on the reverse side of our business cards, which we hand to departing guests to make posting a review as easy as possible. A few years ago, we went a step further and sent the following email to select guests shortly after their visit:

Dear _____

Thank you for staying with us at the Ann Arbor Bed and Breakfast. We hope you had a great time in our vibrant city.

Since most travelers choose their lodging based on online reviews, we would appreciate your taking a moment to click on and post a brief comment at TripAdvisor, BedandBreakfast.com and/or, if you have a Gmail account, Google Places.

In addition, if you have any suggestions on how we could improve your next stay, please reply to this email with your comments.

Thanks again, and we hope you'll choose Ann Arbor Bed and Breakfast the next time you visit Ann Arbor.

Sincerely,

Pat Materka

Pat Materka, Innkeeper
Ann Arbor Bed and Breakfast

Technology continues to evolve, and we now use the review service in our reservation booking service to send out these requests. What we're explicitly saying is, if you liked us, tell the world! If you didn't, please tell us privately so we can fix your concerns and make it better. Emails like these have risks, of course. They could prompt a recipient to post a less-than-favorable review about a negative experience. And even if reviewers mean to pay a compliment, there's no controlling how they'll say it or whether they'll spell it correctly...like the person who commented on our "homely décor."

And there's always someone who will take offense at being asked in the first place. One recipient shot back:

Hi Pat:

I will not be posting a comment about the Ann Arbor Bed and Breakfast. Like many people in today's connected world, my email box is inundated with unsolicited messages. I therefore look very negatively on any business that I patronize sending me *any* unsolicited email. My suggestion to you is to avoid emailing your guests unless they *explicitly* request it.

I did feel obliged to send this gentleman one more unsolicited email. This one was an apology.

✻ ✻ ✻

A positive review will delight me for the minute it takes to read it. A negative review can bring me down for days.

What is it about human nature that inclines us to shrug off praise? When a reviewer writes, "She even accommodated our request for a 7:00 a.m. breakfast," my first thought is, *that was no bother. I'm usually up then by then anyway.* It's not that many of us can't take a compliment; we just can't seem to take it seriously.

But a complaint, let alone outright criticism, feels devastating—all the more so when it's been published on a public website for all the world to see. The Ann Arbor B&B has received more than two hundred and fifty five-star "excellent" ratings and forty four-star "very goods." But it's the ten three-star "average" ratings that grip my attention.

Here are some excerpts:

"My husband slept late and most of the baked goods were gone before he came to breakfast."

"The bathroom had a shower but no tub."

"Breakfast on the balcony was lovely except for the traffic."

Upon such comments, my mind snaps into defense mode. I *want* to say to the wife of the late-sleeping husband: you snooze, you lose. To the bathtub enthusiast: some of our rooms *do* have tubs. Why didn't you select one of *those*? To the traffic critic: Next time, choose a B&B in a bucolic country setting, not one in the hub of a lively city.

Some complaints say more about the guest's unrealistic expectations than negligence at our end.

"Our beds were made each of the three days we were there, but the sheets were never changed."

Does this writer (or anyone) actually change bedsheets every morning at home? Our policy is to change sheets after three nights for guests staying four nights or longer, or about twice a week for longer-term stays. But I don't know of any B&Bs or hotels change sheets on a daily basis. To do so has ridiculous costs to the environment. Changing sheets daily is, in my view, environmentally irresponsible.

Of course if someone explicitly *does* ask asked for a change of sheets, we would sooner comply than argue over the request.

Then we received this review:

> *"The architecture is interesting, but it doesn't have a 'B&B' feel. Basically, I felt like I was staying in an extra room at Aunt Sally's house. It just wasn't quite what I was looking for."*

What *was* she looking for? Who is Aunt Sally, and what's the deal with her guestroom? I'm at a loss. When we're "not quite what you're looking for," but you don't specify exactly what that is, there is no way to know what we could have done to improve your experience.

On further reflection, even an annoyingly vague critique like this one is instructive. If I'm ever inclined to post a negative review, I'll be specific about what I found disappointing. More likely, however, I express it to my host in a private email or in person. In a public forum, I'll stick to the positive.

✾ ✾ ✾

Then there is the dreaded one-star review, rare (for us) but lethal. A one-star review from someone in an uppity mood, who felt somehow offended or slighted, can catapult you from #one to #three rank in an eye blink. And you know this impacts revenue, because many online bookers are going to choose lodging based on favorable reviews. *I* certainly do. And if you're scanning a website and see a cluster of four- and five-star reviews followed by a one-star review, which one do you think will seize your attention?

So one day I was at the computer when an email alert flashed across the screen. "You have one new review!" Holding my breath, I clicked on it. Uh-oh. Instead of the usual "Great Stay," the headline read "This Place is a Dump!" One star. It wasn't a review, it was a rant, and it went on for six paragraphs. Usually complaints are tempered by praise ("convenient location; complimentary snacks and beverages.") But these people didn't like *anything.*

Specifically, they disliked the "exorbitant" room rates, called the breakfast "nothing to write home about," and disparaged the "cutesy" décor. Some statements were false or exaggerated, and I wanted to refute them point by point:

- The temperature that day was in the 80s, not "98 degrees."

- *Of course* our rooms are air-conditioned.

- They had been upgraded to our spacious third-floor room with a kitchenette, balcony, and skylights. How dare they write, "We were put in the *attic!*"

Alas, I couldn't let a bad review devolve in a shouting match. Every one of my responses would have sounded shrill and defensive. And protesting that our top floor room is more like a penthouse than an "attic" would have only given the word "attic" more emphasis.

Fortunately, review sites allow (and encourage) innkeepers to tell their side of the story. We posted this response:

"We upgraded the guests to our largest and most popular room. The entire B&B has central air-conditioning, and the top floor room has a supplemental cooling unit plus two floor fans.

"We are available 24/7 to meet the needs of our guests. Had they mentioned any of their concerns during their stay we would have addressed them immediately. We appreciate all feedback and are totally committed to our guests' enjoyment."

TripAdvisor also provides a mechanism for innkeepers to report a review that they feel is unfair or inaccurate. After stating my case to TripAdvisor, I ultimately succeeded in having the one-star review deleted.

Soon enough, negative comments lose impact as they are followed, and finally buried, by favorable ones. The surprising upside of an occasional three-star review is that it validates the review process. If a business has nothing but five-star reviews, people might wonder whether its reviews are authentic or purchased.

It's well known that it's not possible to please everyone, all of the time. But nothing stops us from trying.

Notes to Aspiring Innkeepers

How to Respond to a Negative Online Review

Innkeepers and TripAdvisor have a love/hate relationship. We love the positive reviews, which lift our spirits and bring us more bookings. We hate the negative reviews which always seem arbitrary, unfair, and without merit.

Fortunately, TripAdvisor, Yelp, Google, and other review sites enable innkeepers to respond to negative reviews and give our side of the story. Do it. It's an opportunity to dilute the complaint, build goodwill, and reinforce your positive image. Here are some tips:

- Thank the reviewer for taking the time to call the problem to your attention.
- Take total responsibility and do not pass the blame to anyone else, i.e., do not say:

  "We're sorry our newly hired housekeeper failed to refresh your room."

  Instead, use the incident to emphasize your priorities and high standards:

  "We pride ourselves on maintaining a clean and comfortable environment. We are sorry for this unusual oversight."

- If a negative review mentions multiple complaints, resist the notion to respond point by point. Keep your response short and positive.
- If appropriate, follow up with a personal letter of apology, again emphasizing your committment to customer service and satisfaction. Offer a refund, or a gift certificate for a discount or a free stay.

Invasion of the Inflatables

When we purchased the B&B in 2003, I figured décor was my bailiwick. I chose the furniture; Bob chose the furnace. I selected the lamps; Bob ordered the lightbulbs. He was in charge of the infrastructure, and I got to embellish everything else.

But like all gender stereotypes, the lines have blurred and the rules and roles are far from static. Not that I was paying attention.

I was so absorbed with the great indoors—fussing over carpet samples and table settings, matching up toothbrush holders with tub mats. Then came spring, and my focus turned outdoors to our south-facing front garden, where I spent hours happily digging and deadheading. Masses of snapdragons and sunflowers, along with three seasons of perennials, bloomed in glorious succession.

But by December, the garden was bedded down for the winter, covered with snow that merged with an equally colorless sky. The B&B looked forlorn against this white-on-white backdrop. That is, until the arrival of—ta-dah—Mr. P, a jolly life-size upright air-blown polar bear.

"You bought a tent?" I said to Bob as he eagerly opened the cardboard box and withdrew several yards of white synthetic fabric. I watched as he plugged in the attached motor-fan. Within seconds, Mr. P (short for Mr. Polar Bear) expanded to full stature—six-feet tall and five-feet across. He wore a snowflake patterned purple sweater and stocking cap and sat back on his haunches with outstretched paws. His smile was pure bliss. Bob anchored him on top of a wrought iron table in the center of the front balcony where he sat like a king holding forth on his dominion below. Cute, I thought, of this temporary adornment. Little did I know, Mr. P was just the beginning.

Inflatables were a new form of outdoor décor that began to appear in the early 2000s, replacing blow-molded plastic reindeer and snowmen. If you weren't browsing through Sharper Image and Frontgate catalogs, they probably escaped your notice. Manufacturers quickly added designs for other holidays; ghosts for Halloween, bunnies for Easter. Trademarked characters, like Winnie the Pooh, Snoopy, and Olaf, made their catalog debut. Soon, we'd own them as well.

When I need to buy something other than groceries, like sheets, towels, or a crock-pot, I head for the mall. There, options are limited, which leads to restraint. Bob, heaven help us, shops the Internet, where choices are infinite. The following Christmas, Mr. P was joined by Santa Claus himself, cheerily waving from a twelve-foot high hot air balloon. Next we acquired a giant Nutcracker, several penguins, and an assortment of snowmen. They joined Winnie and Snoopy, filling the lawn below.

Bob was scrupulous about removing Santa on December 26. After all, inflatable Santa, like the real Santa, had to return to the North Pole to rest up and then resume making toys for the year to come. We wouldn't want to confuse local children by displaying him after Christmas. But the bears and snowmen remained through February. Naively, I thought the inflatable season would be confined to three months of winter.

But in early October, several eight-foot jack-o-lanterns sprouted amid the fall foliage, joined by goblins, ghosts, and a tarantula the size of a bathtub. Most popular was the large menacing black cat crouching next to the sidewalk. He appeared still as a statue, then suddenly his head swiveled as his glowing eyes followed a passing pedestrian. "Did you see that? His head moved!" we heard people gasp. The technology of inflatables design was improving. Dogs walking alongside their owners barked hysterically at the moving cat.

Just as Santa had disappeared following Christmas, the cat and ghosts were removed after Halloween. But the lawn wasn't barren. Bob installed a scarecrow and turned the jack-o-lantern faces away from the street to create a backdrop of giant fall pumpkins. He added an inflatable farmer driving an inflatable tractor. The lawn became nearly as crowded in the fall as it was before Christmas. Thanksgiving approached. At least, I thought, we don't have an inflatable turkey.

Wrong.

In fact, a supplier shipped us two by mistake, and when Bob called to say he was sending one back, the company said "Don't bother. We won't charge you. Just keep it."

Within three years we owned more than two dozen blow-ups including the twin turkeys, and let me just say it: I was embarrassed. I recalled visiting my aunt in central Florida when I was a teenager and making fun of the pink plastic lawn flamingos. Was this display any different? Any notion that our B&B would be perceived as a sophisticated establishment was hopeless.

Our friends felt compelled to comment. It wasn't about the elephant in the room; it was the every-animal-but-elephants on the lawn.

Them: I see you've added more inflatables.

Me, emphatically: It's all my husband's doing. He gets full credit.

Full *blame* was my unspoken message

Bob was dedicated. He rearranged his menagerie showcase, as one would arrange furniture, for maximum visual effect. He bought a scarf and hat for one of the polar bears. When any of the inflatables was damaged (wind gusts can be treacherous), he painstakingly repaired them with duct tape.

Each year, the products got bigger and bolder. On a fall day in 2013, I came home to a gigantic twenty-foot high black Halloween cat rising on the lawn. He had an arched back and upright tail that reached our second story kitchen window. Like our smaller crouching cat (which by contrast looked more like a kitten), Giant Cat had a head that moved and a diabolical grin. I had to admit he was spectacular.

Somebody else thought so as well. Sometime after midnight on the Saturday before Halloween, our deflated cat, along with an especially provocative ghost, was spirited away. It was the first time in our decade of innkeeping that anything of value was taken. Our friend Rick, who owned a fleet of taxi cabs, told his drivers to be on the lookout for a ghost and a very large cat on some lawn across town, but they were never recovered. Some people suggested the snatch was a fraternity prank, but I doubt it. More likely the two were taken outside of the city where no one would know they were stolen goods.

Refusing to be defeated, Bob replaced the cat a year later. Anchored to concrete blocks by ropes and chains, Giant Cat II reigned.

Other holidays do not provoke such mischief. No one has tried to take our inflatable leprechaun (St. Patrick's Day); inflatable eagle (Fourth of July); or the dog wearing a mortarboard and holding a diploma between his teeth (graduation). No one has stolen the inflatable palm trees or the double rainbow.

The display reached its peak in December 2014, the year our three grandsons visited for Christmas. We usually travel to their home in Massachusetts but that year we reversed the tradition. Trevor and his twin brothers Colin and Zach were then aged ten, seven and seven. Bob pulled out all the stops, and wow them he did, with a record thirty-five inflatables. Bears, penguins and snowmen stood toe to toe, like a crowd in a mosh pit. The newest additions were Angry Bird, wearing a Santa hat; Olaf, the snowman from *Frozen,* and R2D2 and C3PO singing "Droid to the World."

As we reached this tipping point, my embarrassment subsided. I realized the excessiveness wasn't the problem; it was the *point.* Their overly ostentatious presence was what made the inflatables funny and fun.

In fact, they have proven to be an effective marketing device. "Which B&B do you own?" someone will ask. When I give the location, they say, "Oh! *You're* the one with the…" Far from mocking us, people go out of their way to say how much they look forward to our seasonal changeovers. I've watched people stopping to take photos or pose beside the inflatables for selfies. I suspect they've appeared on hundreds of Facebook pages.

Some even felt a sense of responsibility. More than once, a passing motorist has called us to say, "Something's wrong with your balloon people!" They were alarmed that the creatures were deflated like puddles; not realizing that the blower fans were on timers because they need periodic rests.

So I've lightened up. My friend Happy Feigleson wrote a book about humor in which she identified its three key elements: incongruity, exaggeration, and surprise. Those words perfectly describe a lawn full of inflatables in front of the Ann Arbor Bed and Breakfast.

I no longer care if people are laughing at us. I know for sure that we're making them smile.

EIGHTEEN

Whatever Can Go Wrong...

It's 8:00 p.m. on a Saturday night in November. Bob and I are having dinner at a new Italian restaurant located within a short walk from the B&B. We are feeling celebratory because we'd only been open six weeks and all nine of our rooms are occupied. A cautious (and premature, it turns out) confidence is settling in. Obviously, this innkeeping business is easy and we are already so good at it.

As we are browsing the dessert menu, the cell phone rang with a call from the B&B. It is Allyn, our student assistant, who we had left in charge for the evening. Allyn is quiet and composed by nature, but right now, she's barely speaking above a whisper. It seems there is a couple—let's call them Mr. and Mrs. Link—standing before her, ready to check in. They're holding a computer print-out of their reservation confirmation for that night, for our Rainforest room. But that's impossible. Rainforest is already occupied, and as I just mentioned, the B&B was full. There were no other rooms available.

Check, please!

✿ ✿ ✿

You may think that the biggest problem that an innkeeper can face is not having enough bookings, but you would be wrong. The real calamity is having one booking too many.

Racing back to the B&B—grateful that it was a block away rather than thirty miles from the restaurant—we approached the Links, who were still standing in the foyer clutching their rolling suitcases. "I can't imagine how this could have happened," I said, knowing the point was irrelevant. It didn't matter how the booking was not recorded. The situation did not call for excuses, it needed a solution. It certainly wasn't Mr. and Mrs. Link's mistake, and they had the sheet of paper to prove it.

Blathering apologies, we asked Allyn to call our nearby competition, the fourteen-story Campus Inn. Why yes, they had one room available—their luxury penthouse suite. It was twice the cost of our rooms. We snapped it up, supplying our credit card to cover the difference in room rates. Since the Links had arrived by taxi, Bob escorted them to our car and drove them the three-block distance to their new lodging destination. Next week, I decided, I'd write them a personal letter of apology and enclose a gift certificate.

Except, of course, the missing Links were not in our reservation system. Or if they were, their names had been somehow deleted. The Campus Inn would have recorded their address, but of course their privacy policy prevented them from sharing it.

To this day, I don't know how we managed to double-book the Rainforest room. I'd like to say it was because we were still in the early weeks after opening, still learning to master the reservation software. That could imply that after few glitches and a brief bumpy start, everything about this business has run smoothly ever since.

Ah, if only that were the case, this chapter would now be ended.

For example, it was only last April that four of our favorite repeat guests experienced the same blunder. John and Marcia Lowenstein, together with Marcia's sister Beryl and her partner Charles, have visited at least twice a year for their granddaughters' birthdays. The girls, Ruby and Jasmine, take turns staying overnight at the B&B and their parents join us for breakfast. I attended Ruby's Bat Mitzvah. We've come to think of the Lowensteins as family.

Yet here they stood, ready to unpack for a long-planned three-day weekend, only to find out we had no record whatsoever of their reservation and no rooms available.

Unlike Mr. and Mrs. Link, the Lowensteins had not received a confirmation. That didn't concern them; after all, they'd stayed with us so often, they assumed we didn't bother to send it. They did not need yet another message stating our policies and protocol. But in fact, the reservation had never been entered. How did it fall through the cracks?

Sorting out what had happened, we deduced that apparently during their fall visit, Marcia said something like, "we'll be back April 10th." "Great! We look forward to seeing you then," I undoubtedly responded. Perhaps I thought she was referring to a previously made booking, and Marcia thought she was making a verbal reservation at that moment. In any case, neither they nor we converted this cheery exchange into an official reservation.

Once again, we found the Lowensteins other accommodations and urged them to still join us for breakfast. The story just goes to illustrate that we show no favoritism to strangers. We can screw up as thoroughly for friends.

Fortunately, most people are understanding. Recalling my Top Ten List of Reasons for Being an Innkeeper: Number one is of course...the people. Consistently interesting and appreciative, they enrich our lives.

Except when they aren't and they don't.

Catering to the Cantankerous

I've yet to see guests arrive in high spirits and then immediately become angry or offended. They're usually cranky from the onset.

"Where's your elevator?" demanded the squat peevish woman as she walked through the doorway and stood at the foot of our stairs. "Well, this is our home," I began, expecting she'd realize that most private homes are not so equipped. "Why didn't you book us in a normal hotel?" she turned and complained to her husband. "You know I don't like stairs."

This was not off to a good start.

"We can change the room you selected to one on the first floor," I offered, adding that I'd be willing to deliver breakfast to the room. She considered this option versus retaining the second floor room that was on the same level as the dining room, the living room with its DVD library and fireplace, and the ready access to free snacks and beverages. Weighing the advantages, she assumed a martyred look and huffed up the stairs, in search of a cookie. She wasn't disabled, just disgruntled.

Encounters like this stand out because they are so rare. We've never forgotten the couple who walked in, took one look at our assistant innkeeper's bicycle in the foyer, and stomped out, declaring that they "were not going to stay in a student flophouse."

Then there was the doctor and his wife from Miami who arrived with their teenaged son to tour the university campus. I already sensed some tension as we ran their credit card but didn't take it personally. Maybe they were tired from traveling. I set out to win them over. "Help yourself to coffee, some fruit, or a cold beverage. Here is a map of downtown and the campus. Would you like any restaurant suggestions? Do you need the Wi-Fi code?" Then I led them up the stairs to Maine Woods, our most spacious and popular room that features a kitchenette, balcony, and a vaulted ceiling with skylights.

Now it's true that it was a little warm that August afternoon, and heat rises. The skylights were open, competing with our central air conditioning. It dawned on me later that in Florida, homes and buildings tend to be hermetically sealed and chilled to about sixty-five degrees, year-round.

"This is unacceptable," the wife stated. Her husband and son stared at the floor, suggesting they were used to her pronouncements.

I, however, was blindsided. How do you respond to such a flat-out rejection? My first impulse was to ask, "Why? What's wrong? Everyone loves this room!" And then hurry to second-guess the problem. "Is it too warm? I can turn up the air conditioning. Let's shut the skylights and turn on the fan."

No, defensiveness was futile. When someone is this adamant, it's best to cut your losses. Why expend energy on trying to convince someone whose mind is made up (and whose dour attitude might infect the other guests)? Better to swiftly and agreeably refund the money.

Because the bottom line is, we just want our guests to be happy, even if it means being happy somewhere else.

There's No Such Thing as a Mistake

...There are only valuable learning experiences.

After the event just described, we made certain to cool down the upstairs rooms several hours before the guests were expected. It's as important to check that the air conditioning (and heat) vents are working properly as it is to refill the candy dish.

Notes to Aspiring Innkeepers

"Spend a night in each of your guest rooms" is advice well taken. You need to live in a room, not just survey it from the doorway, to discover ways to make it more comfortable. It's only after you've settled under the covers that you realize the bedside table is too small to accommodate the lamp, the radio alarm clock, your bedside reading, your reading glasses, and your glass of water. You prop open your book, only to find that the hexagon lampshade casts a dark shadow across its pages. However, the same lamp also spotlights a large spider web in the corner ceiling, overlooked in the daytime. You're also more likely to notice that the shower curtain liner needs replacing when you view it from *inside* the shower stall.

These are the little things that go wrong at a B&B, or within any building or business. Most have no more consequence than a burned-out lightbulb, easily replaced by one of the spares you keep in the supply closet. Or at worst, a quick trip to the hardware store. Or, in the case of the lactose-intolerant guest and the expired carton of soymilk, a trip to the supermarket.

More ominous are the big breakable things that are part of the infrastructure—the plumbing, the furnace, the Internet, the major appliances. In other words, anything that needs to be turned on, plugged in, or flushed.

It Takes a Village

Some people are phobic about airplanes or insects. I live in fear of a backed-up toilet.

As I previously mentioned, for the first thirty years of marriage, we lived in a house with one bathroom. Our 1842 farmhouse had hand-hewn beams, pine plank floors, and heaps of rustic charm. And, I repeat, *one* bathroom. You really want to keep up an active YM/YWCA membership when you live in a house with one bathroom.

So you'd think I'd feel more secure, living in a B&B with, count 'em, twelve bathrooms. Wrong. I feel twelve times more vulnerable. Some of the fixtures are as old as the building, which is now more than fifty years old. So it's no surprise we call the small family firm called Sinks To Sewers on a regular basis. We should put them on retainer.

The company knows our plumbing intimately, every pipe, drain, and faucet. Pat, the matriarch, fields the phone calls and relays our alarm to her sons Eddie or Brian, whoever can best fit us into the queue. If it's a more complicated crisis, she'll send Ed, her husband. He is a wizard of water, able to fix anything.

Now, Ed is a talker. He'll spend five minutes replacing a valve and fifteen minutes explaining to you exactly, in excruciating detail, how he did it. I'd rather hear about his family vacation. But Ed is a professional and he loves to talk about his craft. He wants his customers to understand the precise nature of the problem and how he resolved it. A side effect of Ed's expertise is that I now know more than I ever wanted to know about the drain clearing process. Murphy's Law states:

- Plumbing problems always occur in rooms that are occupied, never in those that happen to be vacant.

- Smoke detectors will alert you to weak batteries by chirping at 3:00 a.m., not at 3:00 in the afternoon.

- And, just as the furnace is sure to break down on a November football weekend (emphasis on weekend, when hourly repair fees are higher), the air conditioning will stop functioning during the university's move-in at the end of August. That's when it's ninety degrees, and each of our rooms contain two stressed-out parents who spent the day unloading a van full of furniture, books, household supplies, and clothing for their returning student.

Joe was the local guy who maintained our heating and cooling. It was indeed ninety degrees and humid, indoors and out, when he arrived to assess our nonworking air conditioner. I was more concerned about our sweltering guests than the hundreds of dollars it might cost to replace the central air conditioning. Joe solved the problem at a glance. "Something popped the circuit breaker," he said sardonically. "I've re-set it."

Sixty dollars for a service call that took sixty seconds? To flip a switch? Hey, he spotted it. We didn't. Joe shoehorned us into a heavily-scheduled work day among five other jobs. I was nothing but grateful.

We had the opposite problem when the ceiling fan in the Rainforest room took on a life of its own, whirling away into infinity. We kept pushing the remote control button but it simply went faster. Instead of gently stirring the air, it created a windstorm.

We reached Amy, our electrician, just as she was about to embark on a sailboat 200 miles north on a lake. No problem. She knew the wiring of our B&B so well that she was able to call in an assistant and talk him through disconnecting the fan's circuitry. When one of our electric water heaters stopped working, Amy drove over at 11:00 p.m. to fix it. Every time we changed a room or floor space, she arrived to reconfigure the wires and switch plates. She also expertly linked the eighteen integrated smoke detectors.

Be prepared for a sudden loss of electricity. Supply all bedside tables with a flashlight and all the rooms with a battery-operated lantern device.

These small family-run companies have somehow managed to provide same-day service, sometimes within minutes of our call, with the dedication of EMTs. Contrast this experience with a much larger appliance repair organization with no local competitors. The washing machine had stopped working mid-cycle, leaving a mess of soggy towels standing in ten inches of water. "Sorry, we can't take your call right now," trilled the recorded message. "Please hold for the next available representative." *Signal annoying music.* "Your call is important to us. Please continue to hold." *Resume music.*

Finally, I reached a live human, who told me that the next available appointment would be three weeks from tomorrow.

To the average homeowner, a non-functioning clothes washer or dryer is a nuisance. To an innkeeper with fifteen guests leaving that morning and eighteen more checking in, it's a borderline crisis. To prevent such emergencies, we now own three washers and three dryers. If there were space in the kitchen, I'd have two dishwashers as well.

The backup appliances were of no use, however, the night that we lost all electricity during a violent thunderstorm. Having to hand wash dishes was trivial compared to being without lights, TV, or the Internet. Lesson learned in the blackout: Stock every room with more than just a flashlight. Each now has a battery-operated lantern, the kind used for camping. Life can turn primitive in an instant.

Despite All Good Intentions

We feel terrible when things go wrong and diminish our guests' experience. Granted, the regional blackout wasn't our fault, but as I look back other breakdowns seemed preventable. Like the time when the hot tub in Ocean View, which usually emits a soothing, bubbling sound, began roaring like an approaching freight train. We weren't pleased to spend $400 replacing the motor, but felt worse about letting down Paula and Jeff, who had chosen the room weeks before to celebrate their tenth wedding anniversary. We apologized and tried to appease them by reducing the room charge and offering a bottle of wine, but it's hard to fully compensate for the disappointment. A glass of chardonnay is simply not the same as a soak in the hot tub.

My first thought in these situations is how the situation might have been worse. I hated contacting Paula and Jeff the day before their anniversary to alert them that the hot tub, an integral part of their celebration, was not working. But it would have been worse to inform them on arrival. Or to have them check-in, get undressed, climb into the water, flip the switch, and then discover the malfunction. By getting a heads-up, they at least could decide whether to come anyway, go elsewhere, or reschedule.

Sometimes the guests' bad experience has nothing to do with the B&B, but since they are living under our roof, we get swept into the drama. One Saturday around 10:00 p.m., a pleasant-looking gentleman in his forties confronted me as I was turning off the lights in the kitchen. "I think we've got a problem," he intoned ominously. I braced myself for a complaint about his room and hoped it was something fixable.

Instead he explained, "My wife and I drove in from Royal Oak (forty miles from Ann Arbor) to have a nice dinner with friends. We were looking forward to a relaxing evening with a couple of DVDs and breakfast with you before heading back tomorrow morning.

"But I just got a call from our next-door neighbor informing us there are a dozen cars in the driveway and a lot of noise going on at our house. Apparently our sixteen-year-old saw an opportunity to *p a r t y*."

He decided to warn us that they might be departing earlier than planned.

Sure enough, the keys were waiting on the desk when I got up the next morning, with a wry note attached.

"Thanks for a lovely stay. Had to leave. Daughter burning down house."

Sometimes things can go wrong as a direct result of trying to do right. Fellow innkeeper Jan Davies McDermott of Davies House in Ann Arbor shares this cautionary tale:

"A nice young couple came to my B&B for a romantic getaway. After they left, I noticed an expensive-looking metallic belt had been left behind. I dutifully boxed it up and mailed it back to the address in our registry, enclosing a short note thanking the couple for staying with us.

"After the belt arrived, the wife called to thank me for sending it. The belt was not hers, however. She had not been along on what her husband described as a 'business trip'!

"Since then, if I find something left in a room, I wait for a phone call before automatically returning it. It doesn't always pay to be proactive!"

This seems like an appropriate chapter to lay a common concern to rest. Surveying my collection of antique toys and other memorabilia, guests sometimes ask me, "Don't you worry about your personal things going missing?"

The answer is two-fold:

1. If I worried about this I probably wouldn't be in this business, and
2. It simply doesn't happen. Stealing is not in character for the kinds of people who choose B&Bs as lodging. In fourteen years, nothing pre-

cious has ever been lost or stolen. Our guests don't come eyeing the silverware.

I emphasize "precious," because there are two exceptions: we do lose our fair share of two non-precious items—clothes hangers and umbrellas.

Many a departing guest has taken their shirt, still hanging on one of our colorful plastic hangers, to their car, faithfully leaving a wire hanger behind in its place. I've collected (and recycled) enough abandoned wire clothes hangers to open a dry-cleaning business.

As for the umbrellas, they are stationed by the front door in a large iron hall tree, upright and ready for guests to use on rainy days. But during a typical weather pattern, the rain goes away, and so does any thought of the borrowed umbrella. It's been left and forgotten in a restaurant or theater, a lab, or a lecture hall.

But in the yin and yang of life, umbrellas are often left behind in taxi cabs. When guests needed a ride to the airport, we often called Amazing Blue Taxi. Rick, the owner, has since retired, but a few years earlier, he arrived at our doorstop with an armload of umbrellas that had been left behind in his fleet of taxi cabs. What a gift! Some of the umbrellas were superior to the ones our guests had failed to return. So, on the umbrella score of wins and losses, we more than broke even.

NINETEEN

Expect the Unexpected

"What has surprised you the most about running a bed and breakfast?" asked Lila as she buttered a second piece of toast. She's an outgoing woman of about fifty, staying with us while visiting her son and daughter-in-law and their new baby, her first grandchild.

Smiling at her, I'm thinking, *I am surprised that you've come to breakfast wearing pajamas and slippers!*

Really, if she were staying at the Sheraton, would she enter the hotel dining room in her bedclothes?

But at our B&B, this happens every so often and I'm not offended. The comment we hear most frequently is, "this place feels just like home." So why shouldn't guests behave exactly the way they do in their own home?

At least she's presentable. My fellow innkeeper Sarah once heard noises at 2:00 a.m. and encountered a naked man in her kitchen, peering into the open refrigerator. The appliance beamed like a spotlight across his crouching body. "This is *not* acceptable," Sarah declared, managing to keep her cool. The man scurried back to his room and avoided eye contact when he checked out the next morning.

Online reservation systems typically have a space for guest memos such as "add extra bed" or "allergic to tree nuts." Next to this gentleman's name, Sarah wrote, "Do *not* rebook" with underlines and exclamation points.

Getting back to Lila's question, here's how I actually responded:

"I'm surprised that I continue to be surprised."

In many respects, the B&B business had become predictable, with each day unfolding like the one before it. Start coffee, fetch morning newspaper, fill the juice pitcher, and set out the sliced butter and bread by the toaster.

Greet each arriving guest with a perky "Good morning! Help yourself to the fruit and cereal. Would you like something hot? There's French toast in the oven, or I'm happy to make you any kind of eggs or an omelet."

My life could be a version of *Groundhog Day,* the film in which Bill Murray's character reawakens each morning to his clock radio, with Sonny & Cher crooning, "I've Got You, Babe."

I could predict which chocolates in the candy bowl would run out first, (*Butterfingers*); how long it would take the green bananas to ripen, (a day-and-a-half); and how much Best Way would charge us for cleaning the carpets ($265, after the 20 percent discount).

But life here becomes unpredictable once you bring people into the mix, and by people I mean guests. It starts with their arrival time. Our website says, "Check-in is from 3:00 to 7:00 p.m.," but that turns out to be merely a suggestion. Incoming guests arrive at their own convenience, sometimes as early as 8:00 a.m. to make use of our free onsite parking. Their room may not be ready, but they are welcome to leave their car, drop off luggage, and pick up a key. Others, often owing to a traffic or flight delay, may appear after midnight. We tell these folks to look for a key in an envelope under the doormat and then signs pointing the way to their room.

Slow Shows and No-Shows

The envelope under the mat system worked flawlessly for thirteen years until the night it did not. The doorbell sounded at 1:00 a.m., the ultimate rude awakening. Throwing on jeans and a sweatshirt, I dashed down three flights of stairs, more anxious to prevent a third ring of the bell, which would surely wake up every guest in the house, than to greet the late arrival. There stood Ryan, a fellowship candidate visiting the College of Engineering, apologizing profusely. "I was told to look for a key under the mat," he said. "But nothing was there." I apologized as well and showed him his room, explaining that Katie, our new employee, must have forgotten to leave it.

The next morning, Katie assured me that she certainly *had* left the envelope. What had become of it?

It turned out that an earlier guest, Joanna, had also been told to "look for an envelope under the mat if you are arriving late." Joanna arrived at 8:00 p.m., which is not "late" by my standards, but she looked under the mat instead of ringing the bell. There she found an envelope, shook out the key, unlocked the door, and quietly walked up the stairs to Rainforest, the room that was specified on her confirmation sheet. She had overlooked Ryan's name on the envelope and the letter inside that began, "Ryan, welcome."

Surprises like this are mere hiccups, no cause for alarm. The late night doorbell cost barely a few moments of sleep. Other mishaps have proven more expensive.

Two couples—let's call them Smith and Jones—had booked two rooms for the last weekend in January to attend the annual Ann Arbor Folk Festival. Our B&B always fills up for this popular two-day event and we count on the revenue spike it produces during the slow winter season.

The Smiths and the Joneses had been coming to the festival from Toronto every year for five years. Each year upon departure, Mary Smith gave us her credit card to hold the same pair of rooms for the following year. Usually if someone books a room several months (or in this case, a year) in advance, we contact that person two weeks ahead of time to be certain their plans have not changed. But these two couples had established such a reliable pattern I failed to check ahead and confirm they were coming.

I came to regret that lapse when 8:00 p.m. approached and the rooms were still empty.

"Maybe they were running late and decided to go straight to the auditorium," I said hopefully.

"Not likely," Bob replied. "They would have let us know."

So I called the number we had on file, reaching Mary on the third ring. It was clear from her bleak tone of voice she'd forgotten the concert. "I've had a terrible year," she said. "Bill and I are no longer together. I lost my job, and last month my house was broken into. I canceled my credit cards since my purse was stolen, so the card number I gave you to hold the two rooms is no longer valid. I have no money to pay you."

What could I do? I did not even ask about the second couple, their friends whose names were not on file and were clearly not coming. We had lost $800 with no chance to fill the last-minute vacancies, but it seemed to me that Mary Smith was dealing with greater losses. Even if I could have enforced our cancellation policy, I had no heart to do so. File this under Cost of Doing Business.

The reality is that even reservations made recently hold no guarantee. Some guests do not note an arrival time, so by 10:00 p.m. we're still waiting and wondering. Did they decide to go to dinner first and forget to tell us? I might phone the absent guests to clarify their status, but often the phone goes straight to voice mail. No-shows are worse than last-minute cancellations because of the uncertainty. All I can do is tape a note on the door, place a welcoming letter and key under the mat, and post prominent signs with the guest's name and arrows leading to his or her room. I sleep uneasily, still bracing myself for that midnight doorbell ring.

Sometimes I get up in the morning and find the key still under the mat, the notes and signs intact, and the room still empty. The reason is nearly always the same. "Don't you remember? I canceled that room four weeks ago." No matter how perfect the system, some messages fall through the cracks and fail to get recorded.

Mistaken Identity

We were out of town on the Saturday that Andrew, our assistant innkeeper at the time, was minding the inn. All but the last room had checked in. Then the doorbell rang, and Andrew greeted a very happy couple in full wedding attire. The bride was wearing a traditional white gown, holding the hem as she walked up the stairs. Her new husband had on a tuxedo shirt, striped pants, and boutonnière.

"The ceremony just ended, and we thought we'd drop off our bags and pick up a key now before going to the reception," they explained, and gave their name, which sounded like "Colby," as in the cheese. Andrew scanned the computer screen and saw "Coadie" registered for the large room up the spiral staircase, known as the Loft. Since the Loft was the one remaining empty room, it was obviously theirs, he concluded. "Just charge it to the card you have on file," the bride instructed. "My mother made the reservation for us as a wedding gift."

Andrew escorted the couple upstairs to their room, which they pronounced to be perfect. They left their suitcases and hurried off to rejoin their wedding guests. Andrew processed the credit card and went into the kitchen to begin preparations for the next morning's breakfast. He felt that serene sense of satisfaction that always comes when the last guest has checked in, and all of the chicks are in the nest.

Thirty minutes later, the doorbell rang again, and Andrew trotted downstairs to answer it. "May I help you?" he asked politely, ready to explain that all the rooms were filled. "I'm Christine Coadie," a young woman announced. "We have a reservation for the Loft."

Andrew felt the blood drain from his bearded face. "Wait here a second," he said, and quickly dashed upstairs, snatched the luggage out of the Loft, and stashed it in the living room. Forcing a smile, he welcomed the "real" Coadies to the B&B, mentioned he had already charged their card, and ushered them to their room.

Who were those other people?

Andrew quickly assessed what had happened. The bridal couple had come to the wrong B&B, and presented a name that he misheard as the one attached to the Loft, the one remaining room.

The dilemma was that he had no way to reach them to let them know there had been a mistake. "I could just envision the scenario," he told us later. "The bride and groom would enjoy a wonderful evening of dinner and dancing, come back here sometime after midnight, climb the stairs to celebrate their wedding night—and find another couple sleeping in their bed!"

Fortunately, Andrew was not alone in his concern. Across town, our fellow innkeeper Marla Queen, was awaiting the two guests who were to occupy her bridal suite. Finally, she called the bride's mother to find out what time her guests would be arriving.

"My daughter told me that she already dropped off her luggage and picked up the key," the mother replied.

"She didn't come to our place," Marla assured her. "I've been here all afternoon."

The mother spoke with her daughter, discovered the error, and dispatched one of the groomsmen to fetch the luggage and transfer it to Marla's B&B, the Queens' Residence. Crisis averted. Andrew's blood pressure returned to its normal level.

It makes a good story despite the anti-climactic ending.

Strangers as Bedfellows

If surprises are going to occur, we'd much rather they happen to us than to our guests. When they do, we hope they can be as adaptable as Jane, in what came to be known as "the taco wedding."

Jane had contacted me six months earlier to inquire about renting our second property for her son's wedding. Since coming to live at the B&B, we had been offering our family home across town where we had raised our kids, the 1842 farmhouse, as a short-term rental through VRBO (Vacation Rental By Owner). I mentioned to Jane that bedrooms in the Farmhouse, as we called it, had king beds which could be split into twins. After canvassing friends and relatives, Jane called back to say she would need more space than the Farmhouse provided and ended up booking all nine rooms of the B&B instead. "It's such a relief to have the accommodations all settled," she declared happily.

Ten days before the wedding, Jane phoned to give us the names of guests who would be staying in each room. "And I'd like each of the king beds set up as twins," she added.

"That won't be possible," I explained. "Our Farmhouse has kings that convert to twins, but the B&B does not. All of our king beds have conventional king pillow-top mattresses."

Long pause. "Oh dear," said Jane. "Many of the people who will be sharing rooms are friends of my sons who have not even met each other." We both contemplated the undeniable weirdness of strangers sleeping in the same bed together. Then, she came up with an idea.

"How about this: you could make up the beds with a fitted bottom sheet, but with two top sheets folded in half along the center, so that the person can slip between the folded sheets and have their own personal space, like being in a sleeping bag."

When I described the plan to our twenty-year-old assistant innkeeper Bailey, she understood right away. "I get it," she said. "Like two back-to-back tacos."

Jane was the first of her party to arrive at the start of the wedding weekend, and I held my breath as she checked on the bed set-ups in progress. If this wasn't what she had in mind, I was not sure what to offer as an alternative. The Farmhouse had subsequently been booked for another event and was not available for an overflow. "This looks perfect," she said with a beam of approval, and went off to oversee arrangements for the rehearsal dinner.

As often happens during weddings and other celebrations, the revelry continued long after the reception had ended. The group stayed up late into the night, laughing and talking on our large front balcony. By the time they finally collapsed into bed, I doubt they even noticed their unconventional sleeping arrangements.

Dodging Disaster

Thus far, I've painted a rather rosy picture of B&B life, one that's both accurate and intentional. This is no cautionary tome designed to warn wannabe innkeepers of the perils of the profession. I like this life. Sure, there is the persistent *un*predictability that's inherent to the hospitality industry, but I find that more energizing than distressing. Guests who conveniently arrive within our normal 3:00 to 7:00 p.m. check-in time are always appreciated, but it's the folks who call from the road and take our last room, say they'll arrive by nine, but show up at eleven, and then mention they need an extra bed set up, and by the way, they're vegan—*those* are the ones who keep you on your toes.

Yet as the months rolled into years, it seemed to me that the B&B business kept getting easier. There were several reasons for this. First, my uber-reliable housekeepers needed zero oversight and kept the place sparkling. That meant that the most physically demanding and crucial part of the operation happened like clockwork. The University of Michigan students I hired as assistant innkeepers were proactive and responsible, not only answering phones but also preparing and serving breakfasts. There is nothing more liberating than learning you are totally dispensable.

We had more and more repeat guests and were scoring high ratings on Google and TripAdvisor. I was certainly not complacent, but I could relax in the expectation that each guest, with few exceptions, would have an excellent experience. And, we were making money. Much of it was plowed back into amenities and improvements, but that was okay. We were creating a welcoming environment, not just for our guests, but ourselves as well.

Five to seven years is said to be the average lifespan for the occupation of innkeeper, from honeymoon to burnout. But when we passed the eight-year mark in 2011, our enthusiasm had not peaked; it hadn't even reached a plateau. If you had asked me, I'd have signed on for another eight years without hesitation.

If you asked our bank, the response would have been, "Sorry, your time is up."

Financial Crisis Fallout

The real estate economy was humming along when we purchased the B&B in 2003. Banks were eager to give us a loan, though not the kind we wanted. We were seeking a conventional thirty-year home mortgage. "It's going to be our residence," we argued. "We will be living there, on the property." The banks rejected this notion, telling us in effect, "Get real. You'll be running a business." So we settled for a short-term loan through the Small Business Administration.

By 2006, local banks were offering even lower interest rates and, in fact, were clamoring to take over our mortgage. Again we lobbied for a residential loan and again were turned down. But, we succeeded in replacing the SBA loan with a five-year commercial loan at a lower interest rate. That meant smaller monthly payments for us as well as proven business collateral for our new bank. A win-win for all of us.

We had sought financing as a residence because residential mortgages last thirty years. Our $800,000 commercial loan would end in five. No problem, we figured; in 2011 we would simply renew it. Like millions of others, we never imagined the colossal collapse of the American financial system in 2008. As the trouble unfolded, our bank notified us that our commercial loan (like many others) would not be extended. Soon we would have to repay the entire mortgage note. We met with other banks and the response was the same. In the wake of an economic crisis that ranked second only to the Great Depression, banks were no longer lending money to small businesses like ours. Period.

So at the beginning of 2011, we had two choices: sell the B&B, or face foreclosure.

It was beyond ironic. The business was flourishing. Our occupancy rate was over 70 percent, compared with an average of 50 percent across the industry. Our annual gross revenue was a healthy $360,000. Among B&Bs in Ann Arbor, we were ranked #1 on TripAdvisor and had a five-star Google review rating. I felt like the star employee who had just set a new company sales record, only to be handed a pink slip and told, "Thanks for your service. You're fired."

Reluctantly, we put the B&B on the market. Surely there were droves of retirement-aged (and younger) couples seeking a large, lucrative B&B located next to a major university in a vibrant city. In our optimistic moments, we reasoned that if the B&B sold at our asking price, or close to it, we'd be okay. In Michigan, any residence can become a bed and breakfast. No special zoning is required. Maybe we could find a viable house to rent and convert it to a smaller "boutique" inn. We would notify our past guests of the new address, and they would loyally flock to our new venue.

If we sold the building to someone who wished to continue running the Ann Arbor Bed & Breakfast, we would agree to a non-compete clause. By Michigan law, a non-compete agreement is limited to one year, and at that point, we'd get back in the game. Anticipating our future moves, we secured rights to the name we'd give our next B&B, the "Ann Arbor Downtown Inn." We might lose the building, but we were not giving up on the business.

All of our plotting was hypothetical, however. As the spring of 2011 rolled into summer, we received very few inquiries and no offers, even though we were listed with one of Ann Arbor's top realtors. We also marketed the property under "B&Bs for sale" on BedandBreakfast.com, a national industry website, but our prime location and revenue record attracted no inquiries or interest.

Looking back, this wasn't surprising. It is well known in the industry that it can take years to sell a bed and breakfast. The economy had not recovered by the late summer of 2011, especially in Michigan. Any would-be innkeepers would likely have to first sell homes of their own. That would be a challenge, with banks unwilling to issue mortgages.

Prospective buyers would face the same problem in obtaining financing to buy the B&B. Since banks were refusing to give loans, entrepreneurship was at a standstill.

Trouble Eclipsed by Tragedy

I hated having a "For Sale" sign on my front lawn. Not only did it fail to attract the casual drive-by motorist, (and really, what were the odds?) but it also confused our guests. Didn't we like running the B&B? Why were we selling it? What were we planning to do instead? Usually I tried to allay their concern by insisting no change was imminent. But to the long-time repeat guests who I now counted as friends, I shared the truth: We loved the business but were being forced to sell because our loan was due at the end of 2011 and could not be renewed. They responded with empathy. Everybody had stories related to the financial collapse and its life-changing consequences.

It was a stressful time, one that called upon my full reserves of denial and optimism. One welcome distraction in 2011 was our long-planned family trip to Disney World, a happy place we had visited seven times as our kids were growing up. My daughter Shannon and son Marc remained close, though their lives were very different. Shannon and her husband Kevin lived in western Massachusetts with three active little boys. She is a lively auburn-haired middle school math teacher and Cub Scout den leader, organized and over-committed, with a zillion interests ranging from genealogy to needlework. Marc, blond before shaving his head, remained single, self-employed, dedicated to his work, his clients, and a vigorous social life. Like us, he was excited that his four-year-old twin nephews and their seven-year-old brother were finally old enough to explore the Magic Kingdom. After months of planning, our extended family convened in June at a Disney World resort in Florida.

We enjoyed a morning of rides and recreation, and then most of our group returned to their rooms for naps. Marc said he'd meet up with us later and went to one of the large outdoor pools. While swimming, he apparently suffered a neurological incident of some sort. By the time the lifeguards noticed something was wrong, they were unable to resuscitate him. He was taken to a nearby hospital, where he was placed on life support.

Since none of our family had been at the pool while Marc was there, and we had separate accommodations within the resort, it was not until evening that we learned that the man rumored to have drowned that afternoon was in fact, our son. During three days that followed, Marc never regained consciousness.

He passed away at age thirty-eight on June 30, 2011.

Looking back on this event years later, it still seems surreal. Because Marc made his living as a painter and remodeler, he was the one who transformed the bland white walls of the B&B with vibrant colors and bold accents. He reconfigured rooms to make them more spacious, rebuilt the outdoor patios, and updated the bathrooms with modern walk-in showers. He created the quirks: half logs on the walls of Yellowstone and an arch painted to resemble a breaking wave over the bed in Laguna Beach. He had touched every corner of the B&B with his creativity and talent.

Marc lived a full, generous, and joyful life, blessed by literally hundreds of friends. More than two hundred gathered for a memorial service that summer, some traveling from the east, west, and Gulf coasts. Bob captured the event and Marc's life on a memorial website he created, marcmaterka.com. Shannon constructed a shadow box displaying photos of him and some favorite belongings. His friends posted photos of themselves sharing good times with him on Facebook. Each of us endeavored to think of his thirty-eight years as a fulfilled life instead of one that was entirely too short.

I insistently felt, and even now feel, he's still with us.

Careening Downward

Meanwhile, each day brought us closer to an unsettled and unsettling future.

By late fall we had two prospects. A local family had approached us about taking over the business, and the U-M Alumni Association was exploring purchasing the building to host visiting dignitaries. The negotiations were promising but plodding. Both prospective buyers engaged attorneys, who each made numerous calls to our attorney. The lawyers chatted away amiably with one another as the clock ticked and our legal fees mounted. No offers were finalized.

We did not remain passive and patiently hope for the best. Together we drew up a list of eighty-five friends and acquaintances we believed had the financial wherewithal to lend us money and the spirit to see it as a profitable investment. Here's an excerpt from the letter we sent in November 2011 to those prospects:

> We are writing to update you on the status of our efforts to sell the Ann Arbor Bed & Breakfast and more crucially, to refinance and maintain the business until a sale takes place. Over the past twelve months we have had interest from several individuals and organizations, but no concrete offers. Given the financial climate and the size of our property, this isn't surprising. It can take two or more years to sell a 6052-square-foot bed and breakfast.
>
> Our revenues are strong, with occupancy still over 70 percent, the average daily rate (ADR) at $151, and the twelve-month gross is over $360,000. We continue to be ranked #1 on TripAdvisor and have a five-star rating on other review sites.
>
> But our five-year commercial loan comes due at the end of December, after which our bank will foreclose. We are turning to you in our effort to privately refinance the property until it is sold.
>
> We are offering seven percent interest for five years to a limited number of investors. The note will be secured by a first mortgage on

the property that was appraised in 2006 at $1.54M. A fresh appraisal is in process. By completing a subscription agreement, you will be investing in a solid property backed by the strong cash flow of the Ann Arbor Bed & Breakfast, and earning a high rate of return.

The letter received a positive response. Most of it read something like "wish we could help and here's why we can't..." but a dozen people said yes, offering to invest anywhere from $5,000 to $200,000. The support was so gratifying, but cumulatively, it fell far short of the $800,000 we needed to pay off the mortgage.

The loan lapsed in December and the bank foreclosed as projected.

However, states differ in terms of what happens to property owners in the wake of foreclosures. In Michigan, after a period of weeks, properties in foreclosure are sold at auction. Typically, the lender buys the property, which is what happened in our case. On May 10, 2012, our bank bought the B&B. *However,* Michigan law provides a six-month "redemption period" during which we could remain in business and continue our attempts to sell it. This meant that November 10 was now the final, ultimate, drop-dead deadline.

"It only takes one," is a reassuring slogan when you're trying to sell a house, but it is nerve-wracking waiting for that "one" to materialize. After three months of negotiation, the family who had been our best prospect abruptly dropped out of the running. A group of former Michigan and NFL football players offered us $1.3 million to convert the B&B into a student living/learning center—a deal we readily accepted—but they failed to secure the necessary funding. The alumni group finally made an offer, but it fell short of the amount that we needed.

I pinned new hopes on a semi-retired couple that had stayed with us frequently and were now confiding a longtime interest in running a bed and breakfast. They loved Ann Arbor, were genial and outgoing, and seemed to have the necessary financial resources. They hired a national B&B consultant, an affable and meticulous fellow who spent three days measuring rooms, poring over our accounting records, and sampling Ann Arbor's best restaurants. He sent his clients a detailed analysis of our B&B, which, we learned later, recommended the purchase. Anxiously, I awaited their offer.

They could see that we'd built a strong business. June through August we were bustling with the Summer Festival, Restaurant Week, the Art Fair, and numerous conventions and conferences. As a midpoint for the ten-hour drive between Chicago to Toronto or to Niagara Falls, Ann Arbor was a destination for international tourists. Plus, in 2012's weak economy, people in neighboring towns and states were deferring luxury trips in favor of "staycations" closer to home. Awaiting the sale that would end our financial crisis, I bombarded our B&B guests with my fullest attention. They kept my mind off a past and a future that seemed outside my control.

When Shannon and her family came to visit us in late June, she wanted to reconnect with some of Marc's friends who had come to his memorial service. She'd met them, but not had time to talk or relate in a meaningful way. So on Sunday, July 1, we invited about twenty of Marc's closest friends to lunch in the B&B's large open dining area. Many in this group had known Marc, and each other, since high school and college. I had not had the courage to speak at the memorial service, but on that Sunday I thanked them for their support. "June 30, yesterday, was a sad anniversary," I acknowledged, "but today we have something to celebrate."

Because one year before, on July 1, 2011, Michael Haynes, a forty-three-year-old father of three who had spent the previous six months confined to a hospital bed due to heart failure, underwent successful surgery in Atlanta, GA, and received Marc's heart. (Our family knew that Marc was a registered organ donor, and we had honored his wishes without hesitation.) Two people, including my brother Phil, who had been on dialysis for two years, received his kidneys. Organ donation is anonymous, but organizations like Gift of Life have mechanisms through which donor families and recipients can connect with one another if they desire. Michael and I had exchanged letters and were now in contact with one another.

"Michael tells me that he talks to my son every day," I told the group gathered at the B&B. "He says he wakes up in the morning and asks, 'Well, Marc, what shall we do today?'"

On July 4, 2012, barely one year after the surgery, Michael finished the 10K (6.2 miles) Peachtree Road Race in Atlanta, Georgia.

Down to the Wire

How can I describe my state of mind that summer? While the connection with Michael lessened the pain a little, Marc's absence was still overwhelming. Losing someone you love puts other crises in perspective. I told myself that I'd already been through the worst that could happen; it was time to reconcile to losing the B&B and find a way to move forward. The Alumni Association had grown silent. We suspected, and ultimately confirmed, that they had somehow learned about our impending foreclosure sale. They were now lying in wait to buy it from the bank as soon as the six-month redemption period had expired. It turned out that the retired couple had learned of our plight as well. Why should they pursue a purchase from us when, within a matter of weeks, the bank would be offering the B&B at a bargain basement price?

I gave my housekeepers two months' notice. Martha responded with an empathetic hug, but Sonia refused to believe her job would end. "Something's going to happen," she predicted solemnly. I dared not pin hopes on the fact that Sonia is genuinely a bit psychic. We stopped taking reservations for dates after November 10th and slowly began moving our more personal belongings to the house across town in which we'd raised our children. Thank goodness we still owned our family home, which was then being rented to groups for reunions and family gatherings. At least we'd have a place to live after the redemption deadline.

What would happen on November 10th, I wondered. Would the county sheriff come and evict us? Would they padlock the doors? Would the bank also seize our furniture and clothing? I didn't want to think about any of it.

Meanwhile, we were working intensely with attorneys to draw up the formal mortgage documents and secured notes to present one last time to the list of potential investors. With nothing to lose, we once again sent out eighty-five more emails in September:

> We are writing to inform you of our renewed and final attempt to raise $800,000 to repay the expired mortgage on the Ann Arbor Bed & Breakfast. We are facing a November 10th deadline to pay off the bank and retain the property that has become our home and our business....

The letter was similar to the one we had sent the previous year, specifying quarterly seven percent interest payments and emphasizing the solidity of our reviews, revenues, and occupancy rate. I took care to make the message sound professional and business-like, not pleading. Once again, the effort drew a positive response.

But this time, something different happened.

Half of the investors raised or doubled their positions. "In for a penny, in for a pound," one cheerfully responded. One couple said yes, then backed out, but three new people came on board. A former work colleague, whose husband advised her not to invest when we approached her in 2011, insisted on lending $20,000. Now her husband said, "Make it $50,000." Unbelievably, by mid-October, the pledges had increased until we were within $90,000 of the sum we needed.

Only $90,000. A sum that was proportionately so small yet impossibly huge.

On Halloween weekend, Bob sent off one more email blast to everyone on the list. Did anyone know anyone who would be willing to offer a short-term loan to make up the difference? The loan would be secured by Marc's house, which we had inherited and was about to be sold. A friend who had declined to be part of the group now agreed to the loan. We notified the investors that the goal had been met! Their checks flew to the closing company. On November 9th, *one day* before the redemption period expired, we presented the bankers with a cashier's check for $800,000. They were flabbergasted.

Today, the Ann Arbor B&B is thriving with the backing of fifteen individual lenders. Several are people we've come to know because they are repeat guests; half are friends we've known for four decades. Harley Schwadron, the cartoonist whose illustrations appear in this book, said happily, "It's just like the ending of *It's a Wonderful Life,* where George Bailey believes he has lost everything, and his neighbors and friends rush toward him with fistfuls of dollars and a bucket of cash to save the day."

I feel the same way, as I picture the final scene in which Jimmy Stewart, the star of the film, looks up to the heavens and says softly, "Thanks, Clarence," to his guardian angel.

Michael calls Marc his guardian angel.

Do I think Marc had a hand in this miracle? I would absolutely bet on it.

Recipes

Soon after we opened the B&B, my daughter Shannon secretly contacted our friends and relatives asking for their favorite breakfast recipes, which she compiled in a notebook for Christmas. It was a wonderful gift that I love to read for inspiration. But more often, I scan the refrigerator for what's on hand and make some variation of a quiche or strata.

Quiche for a Crowd

I've offered measurements below, but there's no need to be precise with the proportions or ingredients. The quiche batter can be five jumbo eggs and a cup of whole milk or ten large eggs and a half-cup of cream; two cups grated Swiss or six slices of cheddar. The oven will do its magic and deliver a beautiful quiche.

Serves 10-12

1 homemade or store-bought pie crust

2–3 tablespoons melted butter for sautéing unless you use cooking oil.

2 cups shredded sharp cheddar, Swiss, Monterey Jack, Colby, in any combination to yield 2 cups

1 medium onion, diced and sautéed

2 cups mushrooms, sautéed (optional)

3 to 4 cups coarsely chopped fresh asparagus, spinach, broccoli or any combination of chopped fresh vegetables

1 cup chopped cooked ham, turkey, bacon, sausage or smoked salmon (optional)

10–12 large eggs or 8–9 extra large or jumbo eggs

1 to 1½ cups heavy cream (recommended) or half-and-half

½ to 1 teaspoon salt (I like Lowry's seasoned garlic salt.)

Add garlic, thyme or savory or other herbs to taste

1. Pre-heat oven to 400°.

2. Over medium-low heat, melt butter in a large saucepan. Add diced onion and mushrooms. Sauté until onion is translucent. Line a 10- or 11-inch quiche pan (preferred over a pie pan to ensure even baking) with pie crust, crimp edges. Pre-bake pie crust for about 10 minutes to prevent sogginess.

3. Reduce oven to 375°. Sprinkle the grated cheese in an even layer over the pie crust. Add an even layer of the onion, mushrooms and raw vegetables. Whisk together the eggs, cream, herbs, and salt. Pour over the cheese and vegetables. Top with chopped red peppers or diced tomatoes to make quiche extra attractive and appetizing.

4. Bake for 50 minutes to one hour until the top is firm in the center. Let set for 5 minutes before cutting.

5. For a tasty, gluten-free alternative, line the quiche pan with fried hash-brown potatoes in place of the pie crust.

Laura's Mother's Crustless Quiche

After Laura Langberg, one of my student assistant innkeepers, shared this family recipe, I abandoned the preceding recipe in favor of this one. No guest has ever said to me, "I miss the crust."

Serves 10-12

1. Preheat oven to 375°.

2. In a 10- or 11-inch quiche pan or 10 × 10 inch baking dish, melt ½ stick (4 tablespoons) of butter. Coat the bottom and sides of the pan.

3. Use the same ingredients and proportions as in quiche for a crowd, omitting the crust. Add ⅓ cup of baking mix, such as Jiffy Mix or Bisquick to the egg and cream mixture and whisk thoroughly.*

   Optional: Stir in a 16-ounce carton of cottage cheese, preferably large curd 4%, but low-fat small curd works as well. (Don't use non-fat cottage cheese.) Pour half of the mixture into the baking dish. Layer with cheese, vegetables, and other ingredients as above. Top with remaining mixture and dot with chopped tomatoes or red peppers.

4. Bake for 50 minutes or until firm in the center. Cool to room temperature, then cut in wedges or squares.

5. Quiche keeps well for up to five days in the fridge. Just reheat in the microwave for 30 to 60 seconds and enjoy!

   *Use plain flour, mixed with a pinch of baking soda, as a substitute for the baking mix. The flour gives the dish more firmness, but I've omitted it altogether when we have a no-gluten guest. Then it resembles a frittata.

Baked Eggs in Ham Baskets

I rarely buy processed lunchmeat, but seeing the packages of sliced Black Forest ham in perfect four-inch circles in the supermarket gave me an idea. Wouldn't they fit perfectly in a standard muffin tin, creating a decorative crust for eggs? This struck me as highly original.

I bought the ham and on a hunch, Googled "eggs in ham cups." Up came literally dozens of recipes, all using thin sliced ham as the base layer of an individual egg serving. Click on "images" and you'll find more inspiration in the photos. So I make no claim that my variation is original, but it makes a great presentation.

Serves 12

Spray oil

12 circles of thinly sliced ham

2 cups grated cheese, any kind

10 large eggs

1 cup whole milk, half-and-half, or cream

salt and pepper to taste. I also often add 1–2 teaspoons of Mrs. Dash salt-free herb seasonings

2 cups green, red and/or orange minced fresh vegetables—asparagus, tomato, bell pepper, parsley, broccoli, spinach, etc.

1. Preheat oven to 375° (or if you're in a hurry, 400°).

2. Coat a standard 12-cup muffin tin with spray oil

3. Insert 12 circles of thinly sliced ham. The edges will look ruffled like a flower.

4. Place a heaping spoonful of grated cheese into each ham cup. Whisk eggs and 1 cup of whole milk, half-and-half, or heavy cream. Pour into each cup, fill almost to the brim.

5. Top with a spoonful of the colorful minced vegetables

6. Bake until puffed up and firm to the touch, about 15 minutes. Cool slightly for easier removal. These will deflate, but remain delicious! Serve on a platter lined with green leaf lettuce.

Marcia's Breakfast Crisp

Marcia Rockwood takes over the B&B when we go on trips, and I always know our guests are in for some exceptional breakfasts. Marcia is a gifted baker and chef. The following is one of her staples.

This is wonderful alone, but Marcia recommends offering a medium-sized bowl of Stonyfield Farms French vanilla yogurt, any Greek yogurt, or quark (a soft fresh cheese), for a topping. To be truly decadent, serve with mascarpone cheese or crème fraiche.

Serves 10-12

1 lb. any stone fruit, apples, or pears (about 3 medium peaches is 1 lb.)

Spray oil or butter for casserole dish

2 tablespoons and ⅓ cup raw sugar. (She uses Trader Joe's)

Pinch fresh nutmeg, grated

1 tablespoon and ½ cup all-purpose flour (Use almond meal to make it gluten-free)

4 tablespoons butter (use vegan butter substitute to make it vegan)

½ cup old-fashioned oats

Pinch of salt

½ cup chopped walnuts, almonds or pecans (optional)

1. Preheat oven to 400°.

2. Peel fruit and remove pits, then cut into quarters or eighths.

3. Place in 1 quart lightly greased baking casserole dish. Toss with 2 tablespoons of raw sugar, 1 tablespoon of flour and a pinch of freshly grated nutmeg.

4. In a large saucepan, melt butter and stir in sugar, then add oats, flour, salt and nuts (if used) until large clumps form in the batter. Spoon onto the fruit concoction.

5. Bake 30–40 minutes until the topping is brown and liquid is bubbling. Let cool and serve at room temperature. Serve with a side bowl of the yogurt or cheese toppings.

6. Marcia likes to add a sprinkle of grated or powdered ginger when she uses pears, Vietnamese cinnamon with peaches, and cardamom with apples—feel free to "play."

On a typical breakfast morning, sliced bread (and croissants and English muffins) sit in an open basket for up to two hours. Plenty of it gets toasted, but the remaining slices grow stale at a rapid pace. I store leftover bread wrapped and labeled in the freezer. The following two recipes turn stale bread into robust breakfast casseroles. Best of all, they are assembled the evening ahead, so in the morning you just need to pop them in the oven.

Savory Sausage Strata

1½ cup chopped onion (1 large onion)

3 tablespoons unsalted butter or spray oil

1 pound sweet Italian, pork or turkey breakfast sausage

10 large eggs

2 cups whole milk or half-and-half

2 tablespoons Dijon mustard

½ teaspoon salt and pepper

2 cups Swiss, Gruyere or Monterey Jack, grated

2 cups Parmigiano-Reggiano, grated

1 to 2 cups of spinach, collards or kale (optional)

8 cups of stale white bread, crusts removed, then shredded or cubed

1. Preheat oven to 350°.

2. Grease a three-quart baking dish with butter or spray oil. Sauté the onions until soft in a large frying pan. Add the crumbled sausage and cook until no longer pink. If desired, add the chopped spinach, collards or kale.

3. Butter a 13 × 9 × 2 inch ceramic baking dish. Spread two-thirds of the bread cubes in a layer. Add a layer of onion, sausage, greens mixture,

and most of the cheese. Add the remaining bread, top with remaining cheese.

4. Whisk eggs, dairy, Dijon mustard, and salt and pepper. Pour evenly over the strata mixture. Cover with foil or plastic wrap. Chill in the refrigerator for at least eight hours or overnight.

5. Preheat oven to 350° the next morning. Bake uncovered 45–55 minutes or until puffed and golden brown.

✻ ✻ ✻

Baked Apple French Toast

While this recipe calls for day-old sliced French or Italian bread, sour dough or cinnamon raisin work splendidly. If day-old bread isn't on hand, I slice fresh bread and leave it on a cookie sheet on the counter for an hour or two until it feels dry. If I'm really in a hurry, I'll put it in a warm (250°) oven and let it dehydrate in 10 minutes.

I like to use Granny Smith apples for their tartness, combined with any red baking apples like Braeburn or Ida Red for their color. The peel provides nutrients and color and leaving it on saves time.

1 full loaf of stale French, Italian or other white bread, crust removed, cut into ¾-inch slices.

6 to 8 cups unpeeled, chopped apples, half green, half red

½ cup packed brown sugar

2 teaspoons ground cinnamon

¾ teaspoon nutmeg (optional)

6 to 8 large eggs

2 cups whole milk or half-and-half

1 tablespoon real vanilla extract

1. Arrange the bread slices in a buttered 13 × 9 × 2-inch baking dish.
2. Cover with apples tossed with brown sugar, ground cinnamon and nutmeg. Sometimes I put the apples in first and wedge the bread slices among the apples standing vertically.
3. Whisk 6 to 8 eggs, 2 cups whole milk or half-and-half plus the vanilla extract and pour over the bread and apple concoction, aiming to thoroughly soak the bread.
4. Dust with a bit more cinnamon and sugar, cover with foil or plastic wrap, and refrigerate overnight.
5. Bake at 375° in the morning for about 40 minutes or until the apples are soft and the juice is bubbling.

Naomi's Best Banana Bread

We always have a bowl of fresh fruit for our guests at the Ann Arbor Bed & Breakfast. Bananas are staples and usually the first to disappear. But sometimes two or three remain, and once they appear speckled, (and to me, unappetizing), I remove them to the kitchen to continue ripening. Once soft and black, they're destined to become banana bread. I've found, the blacker the bananas, the better the bread.

Our assistant innkeepers have tried dozens of recipes over the years. This is our favorite.

3 or 4 medium very ripe bananas

½ cup sour cream

½ cup unsalted butter, softened

⅔ cup white sugar

⅓ cup packed brown sugar

3 eggs, room temperature

1 teaspoon vanilla

1½ to 1⅔ cups flour

1 teaspoon baking soda

Pinch baking powder

½ teaspoon salt

1 to 2 cups coarsely chopped walnuts, pecans or raisins (optional)

1. Preheat oven to 350°.

2. Line a 9-inch bread pan with parchment paper. Mix mashed bananas with a ½ cup sour cream.

3. In a large bowl, use an electric mixer to blend the butter and sugar until creamy. Add eggs one at a time. Add vanilla.

4. In a medium bowl, sift together flour, baking soda, baking powder and salt. Add to wet ingredients and mix well. Stir in the banana and sour cream mixture. Add nuts and/or raisins.

5. Bake 1 to 1½ hours or until a toothpick in the center comes out clean.

This keeps well for several days, and its flavor enhances.

Jordan's Apple Banana Bread

1. Add one diced apple, any kind, to the banana bread batter before baking. The apple will give extra moisture to the bread while the sugar and cinnamon topping will create a delicious sugary crust.

2. Preheat oven to 350°. Prepare bread pan and banana bread batter as above, then add the diced apple to the batter and stir.

3. About 20 minutes into baking, top the batter with a ¼ cup of light or dark brown sugar mixed with 1 teaspoon of cinnamon. Resume baking for 1 to 1½ hours, or until a toothpick in the center comes out clean.

Knock 'Em Out
Sunday Cold Buffet

The first time I offered a cold platter, I worried that guests would miss having a hot dish. Instead, they were delighted. "This is so European!" they enthused. I always let guests know that I'm happy to make some-thing hot. The most anyone ever asks for is an easy scrambled egg. This colorful, no-cook dish has since become reliable weekend staple. Because there's something for everyone, including vegans, it's always a crowd pleaser.

Start with a large platterlike the one you might use to serve a Thanksgiving turkey. Cover with red or green lettuce leaves. Then arrange individual stacks or groups of any or all of the following:

Sliced smoked salmon

Hardboiled eggs, peeled and halved

Swiss, cheddar, provolone, Monterey Jack, sliced

Cream cheese, wedge

Tomatoes, sliced or cherry

Cucumbers, sliced

Cold cooked potatoes cut into wedges

Ham, turkey or chicken, sliced, from the deli section

Sliced red onion, chopped green onion, capers, paprika, chopped
　　parsley or other herbs for garnish

Marissa's Butterfinger Cookies

There is nothing as welcoming to guests as a platter of home-baked cookies. The assistant innkeepers welcome this task and enjoy poring over the Internet for recipe ideas. Our assistant innkeeper, Marissa Gawel, was inspired by the mini Butterfinger bars in our candy bowl when she adapted the following from Sally's Baking Addiction, a popular baking website. Sally graciously gave us permission to share it. Check out more of her inventions at www. sallysbakingaddiction.com, *or in her cookbook.*

Makes about 3 dozen 2-inch cookies

1¾ cup all-purpose flour

¾ teaspoon baking soda

½ teaspoon salt

⅔ cup granulated sugar

⅓ cup dark brown sugar

½ cup salted butter, softened

1 large egg, room temperature

18 mini or 4 regular-size Butterfingers candy bars, coarsely chopped

1. Preheat oven to 375°.

2. Sift and combine flour, baking soda, and salt in a medium bowl. Set aside.

3. Using an electric mixer or spoon, blend sugars and softened butter until creamy, then add the egg. Slowly add mixed dry ingredients until combined. Use a spoon to gently add chopped butterfingers to the dough.

4. Spoon tablespoon-size balls of the cookie dough onto an ungreased cookie sheet.

5. Bake 10–11 minutes.

6. Let the cookies cool on the cookie sheet for five minutes. Transfer to a wire rack to finish cooling.

Outfitting the Perfect Guestroom

Every guest needs a place to sleep, a place to sit, and a surface to do some work on. Here are some other points to consider based on our experience and the consensus of other innkeepers:

Bed

- Make a top quality mattress a high priority. We get good reviews for the pillow-top style which combines firmness with plush softness.

- Offer a queen size at minimum, but if you have room, invest in a king. A king bed that can be split into twins offers great flexibility for pairs of guests, such as a parent and teenager. To reset the twins as king, we use a foam rubber "egg crate" topping covered by an additional king mattress pad cover. It's fit for the persnickety heroine of the fairy tale "The Princess and the Pea."

- Headboards add style, but consider eliminating footboards. Beds without footboards are far easier to make up, and guests who are over six feet tall will appreciate the extra space to stretch their legs.

Recommended Amenities

- Small chest or table on *each side* of the bed
- Reading lights on *each side* of the bed
- Desk, table, or other form of work space
- Comfortable arm chair; two if space allows
- Floor or desk lamp to light the chair and work space
- Bench, chest, or folding rack for holding luggage
- Chest (which needn't be large) with drawers for guests to stow belongings
- Alarm clock
- Flashlight
- Iron and ironing board
- Hairdryer
- Two drinking glasses
- Hangers (with clips for skirt and pants) in the closet
- Wastebaskets
- Nightlight
- Guest diary—People love to read what others have written as well as make entries themselves.
- *What you don't need:* In-room telephones. These days, practically everyone has a cell phone.

Amenities for the Common Space

Perhaps we should call it a Bed, Breakfast, and Beyond, because at a B&B, guests are certainly not confined to their room. You, the innkeeper, decide which areas are public vs. private, but whatever you wish to share—living room, parlor, sun porch—you'll want it to be welcoming. The only "musts" in the common space are comfortable chairs and good lighting. But also consider:

- Guest computer with an attached printer (which guests will use almost exclusively for printing boarding passes).
- Guest refrigerator, for guests to store personal food like restaurant take-out.
- Complimentary hot and cold beverages. We have a small refrigerator of bottled water and soda; a hot water dispenser for tea and cocoa, and hot coffee in a thermal airpot.
- Fresh fruit, home-baked cookies, and other snacks. Why confine yourself to only breakfast treats?
- Books. Consider a borrow one/leave one option.
- Magazines
- Local and/or national newspaper
- VHS or DVD library if the rooms have video or DVD players
- Playing cards
- Board games
- Area maps
- Brochures of local attractions
- Phone
- Before and after scrapbook of the room(s) if you've done some remodeling
- Notebook of menus of local restaurants
- A table with "everything you may have left behind or had confiscated by airport security." The most popular item is toothpaste. Our table also contains wrapped toothbrushes, pens, wine opener, needles and sewing thread, pens, tape dispenser, stapler, Band-Aids.

Guest Relations

- Treat every guest as a unique individual, not generic. Remember who they're with, why they've come; ask about the class they're taking, the show they saw last night.

- Be flexible. Offer an extra early or late breakfast. Assure them they can check in early and leave their bags, even if the room is not ready; they can park in the lot all day after check-out.

- Always ask about needs and preferences, such as an allergy to down pillows or request for a vegan breakfast. Be prepared with pantry items like soy milk, gluten-free cereals and breads, egg whites.

- If they mention they love the granola, give them a package.

- Never nickel and dime.

- The room rate covers everything. No $1 for water or extra charge for inviting a friend from a local community to breakfast.

- If someone leaves an item behind (usually a t-shirt or a phone charger), mail it back. No charge. Cost of doing business.

- Charge by the room, not the person. Accommodate extra people in rooms as space allows. (We also simply give extra guests their own room if it is available and expedient, at no charge)

- Offer use of the washer and dryer on request.

- Provide unexpected amenities like fresh-baked cookies and bedside chocolate.

- Treat every complaint as an opportunity for improvement. Empathize with whatever caused a guest discomfort. Never be defensive.

- Hire exceptional staff and make them feel responsible and invested. Introduce them to your guests. Make it clear that they are not just hired help but an intrinsic part of the operation.

- Trust staff to do everything right, but build in a final room-check system where we and they check one another. When oversights occur, simply smile, apologize, correct, and move on.

Every guest encounter—even the rare negative experience—makes life interesting and uniquely rewarding.

RESOURCES

If you are contemplating running a B&B or even hosting on Airbnb, you'll find tons of useful advice in the books below. These three, in particular, cover business-related topics my book does not, including writing a business plan, financial projections, daily operations, record keeping, marketing, and maintenance. They also provide plenty of insight on guest relations and hospitality in general.

Running a Bed and Breakfast For Dummies by Mary White (Wiley, 2009). White is founder and CEO of BnBFinder.com, a leading bed and breakfast directory. Top-ranked in its genre, current, and comprehensive.

The Complete Idiot's Guide to Running a Bed and Breakfast by Park Davis and Susannah Craig (Alpha Books, 2001). Davis draws from experience in rehabbing and running several guesthouses in Provincetown, Massachusetts. Full of tips, warnings, and engaging anecdotes.

So You want to Be an Innkeeper: The Definitive Guide to Operating a Successful Bed-And-Breakfast or Country Inn by Pat Hardy, Jo Ann M. Bell, Susan Brown, and Mary E. Davies (Chronicle Books, 2008). Four innkeepers first published this book in 1985 when the industry was very new. Now in its fourth edition, it has sold more than 70,000 copies and remains a classic.

ORGANIZATIONS

The B&B industry is served by two national organizations which sponsor annual conferences and provide numerous member benefits, including newsletters, webinars, and aspiring innkeeper workshops.

Association of Independent Hospitality Professionals (AIHP)
www.independent-innkeeping.org

Professional Association of Innkeepers International (PAII)
www.paii.com

And don't overlook the vast network of state, regional, and often local bed and breakfast associations throughout the country. These local groups are an invaluable source of information, support, and camaraderie.

ACKNOWLEDGEMENTS

As the people cited below well know, I had a hard time bringing this book to a close. There always seemed to be one more elusive point to be made, one last story I was sure I'd forgotten to tell. I seem to be one of those people who prefers process to closure.

But I must end this now in order to thank those whose input, encouragement, and exasperation ("You're still not finished?!") spurred me onward.

Joan Reisman-Brill read every word of every chapter, many of them multiple times, raising questions where details were lacking, and ever-so-tactfully steering me to better word choices. Joanie kept me from sounding inept where I merely intended to be self-deprecating.

Xujun Eberling started the Nth Creative Nonfiction Writing Circle just when I needed objectivity from readers who were not biased by friendship. This online writers' group helped shape the book's structure and content. Not one of the members aspired to run a B&B, yet they were eager to read about it. Their support was immensely motivating.

And I'm so lucky to be in business in Ann Arbor where my fellow innkeepers are collaborative, not competitive. Thanks especially to Sarah Okuyama, Jan Davies McDermott, and Chris Mason for their great anecdotes as well as support. And to Marge Trumfio, my first mentor, who helped turn a wish into a reality.

So many friends generously read parts of the book and/or encouraged the project. In alphabetical order: Bill Bradley, Bertie Bonnell, Scott Bushnell, Carol Dworkin, Matt Eastman, Dee Edington, Marilyn Edington, Mary Jo

Frank, Linda Grashoff, Glenda Haskell, Jennifer Hobson, Mary Joscelyn, Jay Karen, Hilary MacPhail, Barbara Materka, Jeanne Paul, Judy Phair, Marcia Rockwood, Grace Shackman, Inger Schultz, Pringle Smith, Bonnie Spinazze, Priscilla Warner, and Mary White.

A special thanks to Anita LeBlanc for her skilled and meticulous copy editing, and nationally renowned cartoonist Harley Schwadron, my long-time friend, for his whimsical illustrations.

Weaving Influence is the company that shepherded this book to publication. I am grateful to founder Becky Robinson along with staff Margy Kerr-Jarrett, Rachel Royer, and especially Lori Weidert, without whom you'd be reading this book (if at all) as a Word file.

My daughter Shannon unfailingly supports all of my undertakings and is a constant source of pride and inspiration.

And finally the man I met 50 years ago this April 1, without whom the B&B adventure, let alone the book about it, would not have happened. Bob defers to me as the innkeeper, calling himself merely the "pro-bono part-time concierge," but in fact handles everything from marketing to maintenance. I never knew what SEO (search engine optimization) even stood for, let alone how to do it. And I would not even be writing this now if he wasn't covering the phones.

Pat Materka has been a newspaper reporter, freelance writer and editor, public relations specialist, university administrator and adjunct teacher, alumni relations and development director, author, antique dealer, workshop leader, and keynote speaker. None of these roles prepared her in any way for running a Bed & Breakfast, which just proves anyone who likes people can achieve success in a business that is not just a business—but a lifestyle.

Pat and her husband Bob live in Ann Arbor, Michigan. They are parents of a daughter and son, and have three grandsons.

Made in the USA
Middletown, DE
15 April 2021